SMART
GOLF

S M A R T
GOLF

How to Simplify and Score Your Mental Game

DeDe Owens
Dan Kirschenbaum

Jossey-Bass Publishers
San Francisco

Substantial discounts on bulk quantities of Jossey-Bass books are available to corporations, professional associations, and other organizations. For details and discount information, contact the special sales department at Jossey-Bass Inc., Publishers (415) 433–1740; Fax (800) 605–2665.

For sales outside the United States, please contact your local Simon & Schuster International Office.

Jossey-Bass Web address: http://www.josseybass.com

Manufactured in the United States of America.

Library of Congress Cataloging-in-Publication Data

Owens, DeDe.
    Smart golf: how to simplify and score your mental game/ DeDe Owens, Dan Kirschenbaum.
        p. cm.—(The Jossey-Bass psychology series)
    Includes bibliographical references and index.
    ISBN 0-7879-1062-7 (alk. paper)
        1. Golf—Psychological aspects. I. Kirschenbaum, Daniel S., date. II. Title. III. Series.
    GV979.P75084   1997
    796.352'01'9—dc21   97-17208

HB Printing   10 9 8 7 6 5 4 3 2 1   FIRST EDITION

Contents

Acknowledgments

We are most grateful to our colleagues, including Ron Bale, Linda Bunker, and Elizabeth Johnston-O'Connor, who have collaborated with us on research pertaining to golf. We are especially appreciative of the outstanding efforts of Eddie O'Connor, who collaborated with us on the research that appears in this book. The staff and players at the Winnetka Golf Club, particularly Head Golf Professional Steve Patterson, made it possible and even enjoyable to conduct that research. And we appreciate the support of the Jemsek family for allowing us to use Dubsdread to illustrate how to play Smart Golf. We also gratefully acknowledge the help of the many fine people at Jossey-Bass for making this book a reality in an efficient and highly professional manner. We feel especially fortunate to have had Alan Rinzler serve as our editor. Alan has been remarkably effective, always maintaining a 20/20 view on how to make this book clear and compelling. Finally, Lisa Caranna, ably assisted by Amy Jones, made the process of organizing and translating our ideas into the final manuscript as painless as possible.

Introduction

This book presents golfers of every age and ability with a very simple, easily remembered method for applying the principles of sport psychology to their games. In other words, we are translating the mental side of golf into a simple set of techniques that you can actually use.

Many golfers have read about the rapidly developing field of sport psychology. During the past decade, two major professional organizations and three professional journals devoted to sport psychology have emerged, as athletes and teams from the Olympics to the NBA have begun to profit from this growing body of knowledge. Dozens of professional golfers, as well, have come to rely on consultation with sport psychologists to lower their scores.

But have you actually been able to use sport psychology to improve your game? For most golfers, the answer is probably no. No one has organized the principles of sport psychology in a clear, concise, easily remembered format. Instead, golfers have been offered for the most part such loosely connected, commonsense advice as "be sure to have total confidence" and "believe with all your heart that the shot you are about to hit will be a good one" or "the swing is fourth on the priority list behind the head, the heart, and the stomach." But when you're a high-handicapper or your game is faltering, how do you find that confidence? How can you really improve your head, heart, and stomach during a round of golf?

There is a way. Our method, which we call Smart Golf, is precisely a clear, concise, and easily remembered application of state-of-the-art principles to help you play golf better. In brief, we use the acronym *PAR* to summarize the key elements of the mental side of golf:

P stands for *P*lan.
A stands for *A*pply.
R stands for *R*eact.

All golfers can remember PAR (even if they have trouble shooting it). We explain how to plan effectively (based on skill levels, course conditions, and other factors), how to apply imagery and a consistent preshot routine to improve your focus and concentration, and how to react and adjust constructively, not destructively, after each shot and after each hole.

Smart Golf also provides a way to evaluate your mental game—right on your scorecard. Our simple scoring system offers detail-oriented golfers a method to review each round. A more global approach is provided for more casual or less detail-oriented players. We also show examples of Smart Golf in action, reviewing how golfers with low, intermediate, and high handicaps might play a wide variety of specific holes. Examples, stories, and illustrative comments from players who actually use our Smart Golf techniques and scoring system also help bring Smart Golf to life.

Our method of Smart Golf incorporates the most up-to-date techniques of sport psychology, including positive focusing, zones of optimal functioning, and stress management. Smart Golf has developed over the past twenty years and is based upon published and field-tested scientific research. We have been fortunate to work with dozens of professional golfers and hundreds of amateurs, applying, testing, and evolving our approach. Now we are offering this proven set of guidelines and techniques to you in this first book on Smart Golf. We believe that everyone, at every level of skill and experience, is capable of playing Smart Golf.

Each of the authors of this book is a dedicated golfer and teacher. DeDe Owens, a former LPGA tour player, has been elected LPGA Teacher of the Year twice and is the current president of the LPGA Teaching and Club Professional Division. Dan Kirschenbaum is a professor at Northwestern University, former president of the American Psychological Association's Division of Exercise and Sport Psychology, and a serious golfer. We both sincerely hope that the quality and application of the ideas in this book are as useful to you as they've been to hundreds of our students and fellow golfers.

Chapter One, "A Thirty-Minute Smart Golf Primer," provides an overview of Smart Golf. It gives you the entire system, ready for immediate use in half an hour. Our experience indicates that many golfers benefit from learning this practical approach quickly. You could then read Chapters Two through Six to learn more about the five components of Smart Golf (Preparation, Positive Focusing, Plan, Apply, React) and the research behind them.

August 1997   DEDE OWENS
                                               DAN KIRSCHENBAUM

SMART
GOLF

1

A Thirty-Minute Smart Golf Primer

 *I taught the basics of Smart Golf to six of my students in about 30 minutes. Then we went out and had a group playing lesson. Each of them (golfers with handicaps ranging from very low to very high) benefited dramatically from Smart Golf— and that was obvious from this very first outing. Smart Golf has definitely improved my own game, as well.*

> *Rachel Teresi (1996)*
> *LPGA Teaching Professional*
> *Cog Hill Learning Center, Lemont, Illinois*

Ask golfers about their mental games and they will tell you about expectations, plans, emotional control, anxiety management, confidence, concentration, focus, and many other ideas. When we boil these ideas down into their essence, five factors emerge: Preparation, Positive Focusing, and Plan, Apply and React (PAR).

Preparation refers to the degree to which the golfer is ready to play before the round. Positive focusing is a method of remembering and keeping track of good shots rather than focusing on mistakes while playing a round of golf. Plan takes the notion of course management and refocuses it on the development of an effective strategy to play each hole and each shot. These plans depend on an analysis of the hole's strengths and weaknesses versus the golfer's own strengths and weaknesses. The Apply component begins after you have identified a general target for a shot and have picked out the club that you think will get you there. It includes identifying a specific target and implementing a very consistent preshot routine. The final component of your mental game concerns how you React to your shots and your score while you are playing. Reactions can vary a great deal and still enable you to focus effectively on your next shot. Some reactions, however, particularly negative and very global ones, can distract you from focusing on the next shot, as well as make the game less enjoyable.

Smart Golf encourages you to keep track of (or self-monitor) these five critical elements of your mental game. By monitoring the five elements, you can identify ways of improving them both during your round of golf and afterward. This chapter presents the basics of each of these five elements of Smart Golf. We also describe a scoring system that you can use to evaluate how well your approach to this essential part of the game is progressing.

Smart Golf Scorecard

Take a close look at the scorecard in Figure 1.1 to get an understanding of how to self-monitor the five elements of Smart Golf. This card was used by Dan, one of our students, during a recent round of golf. Note that under the line that includes Dan's name and scores—where the other players' names and scores would usually go—you see a line for Preparation (abbreviated Prep) and Positive Focusing (Pos Foc). Below that line are separate lines for *P*lan, *A*pply, and *R* (for *R*eact).

The system for monitoring shown in the scorecard can allow you to examine which elements of your mental game are going well and which require further attention—while you play. This should help you make adjustments during the round that will have an immediate positive impact on your swing and attitude. An analysis of your total Smart Golf score at the end of the round can help you evaluate your mental game as a whole. Let's take a closer look at each element, based on the example in Figure 1.1.

Figure 1.1
How to Use Smart Golf to Score Your Mental Game:
An Example from the Winnetka Golf Club

HOLE NUMBER	1	2	3	4	5	6	7	8	9	OUT	Winnetka Golf Club
Blue Tees	349	519	157	419	362	413	167	372	407	3165	RATINGS
White Tees	336	501	144	504	346	396	134	361	397	3020	Blue 70.9/125
Par	4	5	3	4	4	4	3	4	4	35	White 69.9/122
Handicap	13	1	15	5	9	7	17	11	3		Forward 68.1/118
Dan	4	5	3	4	6	4	4	6	4	40	Red 73.3/124
(Prep = 1) Pos Foc	46 S6	S S7	7 13 S7	4 S W P	S P E S	W P D	SP		D 8C P	8	Member
Pace of Play	:12	:31	:38	:53	1:06	1:21	1:30	1:44	1:58	1:58	Winnetka Park District
Plan	✓	✓	✓	✓	✓	✓	✓		✓	8	•
Apply	✓		✓	✓	✓	✓		✓	✓	7	Golf Course Superintendents Association of America
Match Play +/- (R)	✓		✓	✓		✓	✓	✓	✓	7	•
Handicap	9	1	15	3	13	11	17	7	5		Professional Golfers Association
Par	4	5	3	4	4	4	3	4	4	35	
Red Tees	314	490	132	383	330	370	118	353	343	2833	

Figure 1.1, continued

HOLE NUMBER	10	11	12	13	14	15	16	17	18	IN	TOT	HCP	NET
Blue Tees	527	386	305	192	346	480	387	221	443	3287	6452		
White Tees	511	378	294	163	330	472	372	209	436	3165	6185		
Par	5	4	4	3	4	5	4	3	4	36	71		
Handicap	2	8	18	16	14	6	12	10	4				
Dan	5	6	4	4	5	6	4	2	5	41	81		
(Prep = 1) Pos Foc	5W 2,3	D	2,3W	SP	5W	7W	7	2,3W	D	9	17		
Pace of Play	2:15	2:29	2:40	2:50	3:03	3:19	3:33	3:44	4:00				
Plan	✓			✓			✓	✓	✓	5	13		
Apply	✓		✓	✓		✓	✓	✓	✓	7	14		
Match Play +/- (R)	✓	✓	✓	✓		✓	✓	✓	✓	8	15		
Handicap	2	6	8	18	14	10	12	16	4		59 + 1 (prep)		
Par	5	4	4	3	4	5	4	3	5	37	72	= 60/74	
Red Tees	493	370	283	123	314	464	364	149	388	2948	5781	= 81%	

🏌 Preparation

Notice in the example that "(Prep = 1)" appears at the beginning of the Pos Foc line. The 1 refers to Dan's view of the adequacy of his preparation for that round of golf. Maximum preparation would appear as a 2, adequate preparation as a 1, and minimal or no preparation as a 0.

A Quick Look at Preparation

The scorecard shows that Dan felt pretty good about the preparation he did. He stretched and hit several balls prior to his tee time. He hit four 7-iron shots and three 3-wood shots, and rolled several practice putts. Dan also spent a few minutes developing a plan for how to play the first two holes, taking into account weather and course conditions. However, he did not have enough time that day to hit other shots on the range (with other clubs, for example) or to practice any chipping or pitching.

Dan would have preferred to hit a greater variety of shots on the range, to spend a few minutes chipping and pitching near a practice green, and to develop a more complete plan for the round. Therefore, he scored his preparation in the "OK, but not great" range, a 1 instead of a 0 or a 2. If he'd managed to fit in everything, he would have scored his preparation as a 2—and if he did not have time to hit any balls on the range, he would have scored it as a 0.

Most golfers feel more relaxed and eager to play

when they stretch and warm up completely before a round of golf. Warming up could include a variety of stretching exercises, particularly for the back and shoulders, and hitting a variety of shots at the driving range. An ideal level of preparation would also include several minutes of chipping and putting. Some teachers of golf emphasize chipping and putting as even more important than hitting balls at the range as part of the warm-up. Indeed, Gene Sarazen—who hit the most famous shot in golf history, a 4-wood for a double-eagle at the 1935 Masters—argued that hitting too many balls prior to playing is wrongheaded:

> In my tours throughout the country, I have observed that less than one percent of our golfers know how to practice correctly. At every club there is a group of over-eager beavers who bang hundreds of balls down the practice fairway and are muscularly tired before they actually tee off. You've got to be fresh to play golf. . . . Before a round, a player should warm-up, not practice. At my age [48], preferring as I do to conserve my energy, my warm-up consists of 15 or 20 shots with my No. 6- or 7-iron [to] check my timing; four or five drives to unlimber my other muscles; and five minutes or so on the practice green [1950].

Scoring Preparation

The important thing is to understand what a good level of preparation *for you* entails. It probably includes some stretching and warming up, hitting balls on the range, and at least some chipping and putting. If you reach your own criteria for a good or better level of preparation, give yourself a score of 2 in the appropriate place on your scorecard before beginning your round. If you reach the "adequate but not great" level, then give yourself a 1. If you do virtually no preparation before the round, put down a 0.

Positive Focusing

Positive focusing is a method of directing your attention to the better aspects of your golf game. This provides an antidote to the natural tendency to focus far too much attention on mistakes.

As in Figure 1.1, put Pos Foc or the capital initials "PF" on the line underneath your name on the scorecard. Then after each hole, do three things: record all good or better shots, mentally replay your good or better shots prior to teeing off, and forget problematic shots while playing.

Record All Good or Better Shots

Write down each shot that was good, very good, or excellent compared to your usual shots. Focus primarily on the quality of the shot. Try to use a lenient standard to define these shots. "Did I hit the ball as I intended and did it go basically where I was aiming?" works pretty well. If you answer yes to this question after hitting a shot, then the shot was at least good. If the shot took a bad bounce but you could still answer yes to that question, then that shot deserves a good or better evaluation no matter where it wound up.

Complete the recording of the good or better shots using abbreviations for the club or shot used on that hole, as shown in Figure 1.1. The "5W" under Hole #1 indicates that Dan regarded his 5-wood tee shot on that hole as in the good or better range. Actually, Dan viewed this shot as very good—he hit it very solidly and it went straight down the middle of the fairway. The "6" shows that Dan's 6-iron approach shot was also in his very good range.

You will notice a variety of abbreviations in the sample scorecard in Figure 1.1. The following are some particularly helpful ones: LP = long putt; SP = short putt; SW = sand wedge, not from a bunker; SB = sand wedge from bunker; 7C = a chip shot with a 7-iron. You'll see other useful abbreviations in Chapter Three, which discusses positive focusing in more detail.

Replay Before the Next Tee

At the completion of each hole, on your way to the next tee, take a few seconds to recreate in your mind's eye each shot that you recorded as good or better. Try to imagine what the shots felt like and looked like. You can begin the image from the point of setup just

prior to swinging or from the point at which you identified a specific target and lined up to that target. Then
try to remember what it felt like when you swung. Also remember what you were thinking about and focusing on. Try to see the ball in flight as you did when
you hit it and remember the feeling of excitement or
satisfaction that came over you. Any systematic way
of replaying the shot, positively refocusing on it, should
prove useful. These replays should take just a few seconds each.

Dan's ninth hole on the scorecard in Figure 1.1 provides a good example of the use of this replaying aspect
of positive focusing. On that hole, he had a sixty-foot
chip shot left to the hole after his approach shot landed
short of the green by about five yards. The pin was
tucked over a ridge and Dan had to negotiate the five
yards of the fringe before landing the ball on the green.
He remembered his decision to select an 8-iron. He also
recalled the smoothness of the swing and the feeling of
solid contact when he hit that chip to six feet below the
hole. He then recalled his setup for the six-foot putt.
He had identified an intermediate target even on that
short putt. This allowed him to line up with confidence
to stroke the putt. Prior to hitting the putt, he focused
on the hole itself. He hit the putt smoothly and right
toward the intermediate target selected. It rolled into
the center of the cup with perfect speed.

Dan focused on these memories, in imagery form,

prior to his tee shot on the tenth hole. He avoided thinking about the 5-iron he mis-hit on the ninth hole—the one that got him into the spot where he required the 8-iron chip shot. He remembered but did not dwell on the fact that he had hit his 5-iron a little heavy. Instead he focused on the details of his well-executed chip and putt, enabling him to feel more confident prior to hitting his next shot. He knew he would remember the heavy 5-iron shot and could consider that after the round.

Forget Problematic Shots While Playing

Try to keep your attention focused on what you did well. You can set aside the problematic shots (as Dan did with his heavy 5-iron approach to the ninth green) and use them for guidance, subsequent practice, and instruction—after the round. If you find yourself struggling to forget problematic shots during play, remind yourself of the challenging nature of golf:

- No one plays perfect golf.
- Problematic shots present opportunities to recover.
- Extra practice and instruction can improve anybody's swing.

Scoring Positive Focusing

Score your positive focusing by giving yourself one point for each hole on which you self-monitored at least one good or better shot, and also replayed at least one good or better shot prior to teeing off at the next hole. You can see in Figure 1.1 that Dan reached these criteria on eight of the front nine holes and all of the back nine holes, resulting in a Positive Focusing score of 17 for that round.

Plan

To qualify for a check on the scorecard under the *Plan* heading for a particular hole, you must follow the four planning principles: personal par, conservation, wide first, and safety first.

Personal Par

Par on the scorecard is a standard of excellence to which we compare our scores for each hole. For example, in an ideal golf heaven, on a par 4 hole, you would hit the green in two strokes and make two putts for your par. Thank goodness the USGA recognizes the inequality of skill among golfers and has established the handicap system. This allows everyone to enjoy the game and measure his or her skills against par.

Personal par takes your handicap into consideration and allows you to approach each hole with a more realistic expectation based on your current ability. Personal par is the par of the hole plus the handicap strokes allotted to you on the hole. Let's use Dan's scorecard, Figure 1.1, to determine his personal par on Hole #4 at the Winnetka Golf Club. Dan's course handicap at that time was 9. Therefore, Dan got one handicap stroke on holes with handicaps 1 through 9. Hole #4 is the fifth handicap hole on that course, so Dan got one stroke. Par is 4. Dan's personal par on the hole was 5.

Use your personal par to begin formulating a plan to play the hole. It helps to know the layout of the hole, but even if you never played the course you will have some information available; the scorecard or yardage marker on the tee often provides a sketch. If so, use it to help you see the overall design of the hole including the fairway and green contours as well as the hazards and out-of-bounds areas. When information is not presented, ask your playing partners about the hole if they have played the course. The rules allow you to use this general knowledge to your advantage. You could also stand on the tee and based on what you see, make your best guess as to the club selection and direction that will most likely avoid trouble. If you have time, walk into the fairway to get a more complete assessment of the hole.

Let's use the sample scorecard in Figure 1.1 and follow Dan's narrative on how he planned and played Hole #4, incorporating his personal par of 5:

I took the #4 hole's handicap very seriously because of the many strengths of the hole. My personal par of 5 would be a good score. The hole actually plays longer than the 419 yards (Blue tees) listed on the card. The fairway is typically soggy and the wind is usually in the player's face. In addition, a long creek lurks to the right of the fairway and a series of large trees guard the entire left side of the fairway.

The ten-miles-per-hour wind in my face on the tee and the sogginess of the fairway made me realize that my better-than-average tee shot with a driver would leave me with a 180- to 200-yard shot into the green on that day. I figured I could get to almost the same point using a 3-wood off the tee. The sogginess of the fairway would negate most of the added distance in roll from the driver versus the 3-wood. A 3-wood also would add potentially better control of the tee shot, thereby increasing the chance of getting the ball in the fairway. Since this was essentially a three-shot par 5 for me, I thought a 5-wood would be better still: even more control and I didn't really need the extra distance from the 3-wood. I could then hit either a middle-iron second to set up a wedge approach or a 5-wood second to set up a pitch or chip—depending on the position and lie of the tee shot.

The tee shot turned out OK, not great. I had a good lie and a good angle of approach. I went for a 5-wood second shot because of my confidence in the club (more than in my 5-iron, for example) and the desire to have a pitch or chip into the green (to set up a chance for a personal birdie 4). The second shot was better than the tee shot. The forty-yard pitch third shot was OK. I sank the twelve-footer for my personal birdie 4.

Conservation

The conservation principle of planning means using more conservative instead of less conservative shots. In other words, use your ability today—not your ability tomorrow (after you become better) or on your best in-the-zone days. Hit shots that you have actually practiced and executed on the range successfully. This approach should conserve strokes.

Wide First

Try to play to the widest part of the fairways and greens. This can reduce your anxiety, increase your confidence, and usually improve your score. Narrow landing areas on the fairways and greens require rather demanding levels of precision in both distance and direction. Remember, the goal in golf is to shoot lower numbers and have fun. You will shoot higher numbers and have less fun when you take unnecessary chances by aiming for narrow strips of the fairway or pins tucked in very challenging positions on the greens. Even the pros generally aim for the widest target areas.

Safety First

When you get in trouble on the golf course, go for the more conservative, safer means of escape. In other words, follow the basic principle: *When playing safe, play safe.* This approach yields lower scores compared to attempting to squeeze extra yards or the best possible angle from difficult positions and difficult lies.

A classic scenario you may have experienced is aiming for a small opening between trees or between branches of a tree when your ball trickles into the woods. If you pull off the shot, you may have a much shorter shot to the green than you would if you hit to an open area on the fairway. However, many times golfers who try for the more difficult shot wind up back in the woods, with a one- to two-stroke penalty for taking a gamble to gain ten or twenty yards.

Do you remember the last time you attempted to escape from trouble and put your escape shot into a bunker, water hazard, or back into the trees? How about the time you were trying to lay up short of a pond and put the ball into the water anyway? Those are very unpleasant memories for most golfers. If you accept penalty situations or lay-ups for what they are, you can decrease your score and add confidence to your game.

Try to stick to your own plan regardless of the advice offered by others or strategies used by others.

This may be quite difficult when your personal par calls for a very conservative tee shot. Remember that you know your game better than your partners know your game. They may go for a big tee shot on every hole. This strategy clearly violates our conservation principle—and yields big numbers on some holes for most golfers.

Scoring Plan

Remember, your plan begins on the tee when you establish your personal par. After that each shot has a planning phase that considers each of the other three principles: conservation, wide first, and safety first. You must follow all four principles for the hole and for every shot on the hole to score yourself with a check under the *Plan* heading for that hole:

1. *Personal Par.* Be realistic regarding your ability to score on the hole.
2. *Conservation* (each shot). What is your ability today, not tomorrow?
3. *Wide First* (each shot). Higher percentage shots increase confidence, reduce anxiety, and improve scores.
4. *Safety First* (each shot). Shots from the fairway are much easier than shots from the woods.

🏌 Apply

This element of Smart Golf takes you from the point of having selected a club to actually hitting the shot. To qualify for a check on the scorecard under the Apply category, you must meet five criteria for every shot on the hole: identify a specific target, use visual or kinesthetic imagery, commit to the shot, complete your preshot routine, and focus on the target during execution.

Identify a Specific Target

In the planning phase, you selected a wide area on the fairway or greens as your general target. Now identify a specific target by narrowing the general target to a small area either in the fairway or on the green.

Visual or Kinesthetic Imagery

You can use visual images, images of the feel of the shot (kinesthetic images), or a combination of both. Use the form of imagery that you prefer. They all can work quite well.

Visual Images

Visual images are pictures in your mind's eye. In golf, you can visualize the shot that will allow the ball to reach the specific target you have identified. This visualization works best when it includes the amount of roll the ball will have and the trajectory of the shot. It could also include an image of the swing you plan to use to produce that shot.

Kinesthetic Images

Images that focus on the feelings of the swing are kinesthetic images. Use rehearsal swings to feel the amount of swing length and pace that will get the ball to the target. (We use the term *rehearsal,* instead of *practice,* because rehearsal helps emphasize the importance of matching the feeling of the swing to the actual execution of it.) Then focus on those sensations by creating an image of that feeling.

Commit to the Shot

It is critical to commit to the shot before attempting to execute it. At this point, you have identified a specific target and have a club in your hand. You must convince yourself that if you swing this club the way you want to, it will get the job done. You want a feeling of confidence in your selection of club and shot before you attempt to hit the ball.

Have you had the experience of dithering between an easy 6-iron or an aggressive 7-iron, then deciding on the easy 6-iron? How many times have you proceeded to half-swing at the ball rather than commit to make a full turn using that 6-iron? Try to formulate a plan and really believe in it.

Once you have decided on the club and type of shot

you want to execute, make one or two rehearsal swings to help you feel more committed. Go ahead with the shot you decided upon and allow yourself to see what happens. If you fully commit, you have a good chance of executing it the way you have planned; half commitments often produce poor outcomes.

Complete Your Preshot Routine

To complete the preparation phase, you need a preshot routine that allows you to align your club and body in a manner that creates a consistent and playable ball flight. A playable ball flight is one that ends up near the target. Figure 1.2 shows three basic playable ball flights. If your predominant ball flight is not illustrated, you may want to get professional assistance to help you develop one. That will help you lower your scores more quickly using Smart Golf strategies.

Many players include rehearsal swings in their preshot routines. You can make these from behind the ball viewing down your target line or beside the ball and parallel to the target line. Whichever approach you take, try to stay very consistent in where you stand and on the number of rehearsal swings you use.

Try to include four elements in your routine as you set up the ball. We suggest the following order:

1. *Target line.* From behind the ball, determine the line on which you want the ball to start,

Figure 1.2
Playable Ball Flights

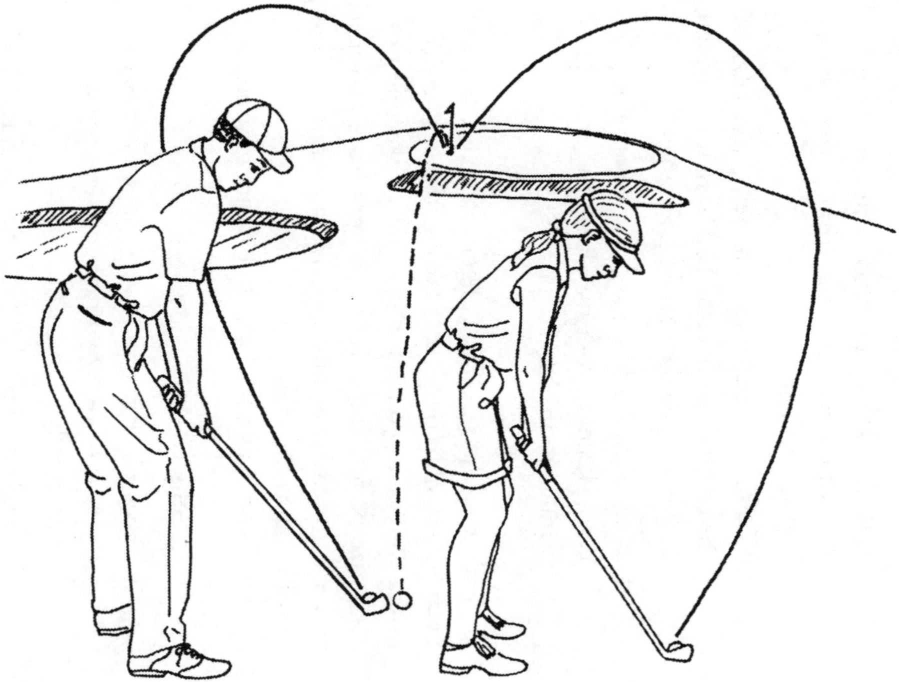

based on your desired ball flight noted in
Figure 1.2.

2. *Intermediate target.* Find an intermediate
   target two to four feet in front of the ball on
   your target line.

3. *Clubface alignment.* Align the bottom edge of
   the clubface behind the ball so that it is square
   to the intermediate target and target line.

4. *Body alignment.* Align your body to the
   club—keeping your feet, hips, and shoulders
   parallel to the target line.

Following this target and alignment phase, you need
a way to start and complete the swing. Use of a very consistent routine to go from alignment to execution can
maximize performance. Routines vary from player to
player. But better outcomes follow the very consistent
use of whatever routine you adopt.

Here's an example of one functional routine:

1. Identify your specific target.

2. Take one or two practice swings to rehearse
   the type of swing you want to execute when
   you actually hit the ball.

3. From behind the ball, identify the target
   line to the specific target in the fairway
   or on the green.

4. Identify your intermediate target. While standing parallel to your target line, align the clubhead first so that it is directly in line with the intermediate target.

5. Rotate your head so that your eyes can move along the target line from the ball to the intermediate target to the specific target without lifting and turning your head.

6. Get comfortable (perhaps with a waggle of the club) and feel ready to execute the shot.

Focus on the Target During Execution

When beginning your swing, the ideal style of focusing places your attention on the specific target or on a feeling that gets you target-oriented. Some golfers also use a mechanical thought to get through the swing confidently. The best mechanical thoughts are whole swing thoughts. These are thoughts that include one or two elements that encourage smooth and complete swings. For example: extend and through; stretch, spring; down and through; turn and through; and arms together, through.

Partial swing thoughts or specific swing mechanics or positions can create difficulties and interrupt the smooth flow of the swing. For example, the isolated thought "extend" or "turn" may leave you focused on the backswing and decrease your ability to swing through the ball, completing your swing in balance. Remember, avoid focusing on hitting *at* the ball, as opposed to swinging *through* the ball. *The aim is to get through the ball, not to the ball.*

It also helps to keep your swing thoughts relatively simple. If you're telling yourself about grip pressure, backswing elements, downswing elements, and target issues while you swing, it becomes unlikely that you will execute smoothly and with confidence. Leave those thoughts to the practice tee.

Scoring Apply

You get a check for *Apply* on the hole if, before every shot, you took the following steps: identified a specific target, used imagery (either visual or kinesthetic), committed to the shot, completed your preshot routine, and focused on the target during execution (with or without whole swing thoughts).

React

The final category for monitoring shown in Figure 1.1 and used in Smart Golf concerns the way you react to your shots during a round of golf. To qualify for a check under this category, you must find a way to stay positive, even in the face of the many challenges that golf presents: *Positively stay positive.*

By following the four *React* rules, you can stay positive as you play: use only positive verbal comments about your game and yourself, defend yourself against negative comments, keep your attributions adaptive, and use the 4-F Technique to stay optimistic.

Only Positive Verbal Comments

Keep all overt comments—the things you say out loud—positive, favorable to yourself and your skills. It's OK to have momentary negative covert (internal) reactions. After all, you are human. But keep them to yourself and quickly replace them with positive comments. If you say anything negative out loud after a shot, you do *not* qualify for a check for that hole under the *React* category.

Defend Yourself Against Negative Comments

If a playing partner makes a negative remark about your skills or golf game, defend yourself—do not accept it. For example, suppose your partner says, "You're just having a terrible time on the greens today!" You can respond with "Everyone misses some of them. They'll start dropping for me." Or "These are tough greens." This defense makes the point to your playing partner (and yourself!) that you believe in yourself and refuse to accept a negative analysis of your game.

Keep Attributions Adaptive

Attributions are the causes you assign to events or outcomes. To maintain your positive outlook, focus your attributions for problematic shots on such external factors as lack of practice or on elements of the course or weather. Avoid attributing poor outcomes to such internal qualities as lack of intelligence or ability. If you hit a shot into the woods, for example, try to view it as a function of not practicing enough or of an unlucky bounce. What sense does it make to call yourself "Stupid!" for hitting a poor shot? Did your IQ drop right before you hit it? External attributions maintain your belief in yourself and help you see problematic shots as temporary glitches, not signs of your basic inadequacies.

Use the 4-F Technique to Stay Optimistic

The 4-F Technique (Kirschenbaum, 1997) helps golfers cope with errors or problems on the golf course. This technique can allow you to transform a challenging and potentially very negative moment into an accepting and optimistic approach. The 4 F's are:

> Fudge!
> Fix
> Forget
> Focus

The first F—Fudge!—encourages you to express yourself, briefly and preferably silently, if you feel strongly about the shot. Sometimes such reactions are unavoidable. You can minimize the potential negativity of the reaction if you simply allow the reaction to occur without feeling guilty about it.

The next F—Fix—encourages you to use a rehearsal swing from the place where the problematic shot occurred. Try to make some change in your approach to that shot and then actually swing to show yourself that you can fix it.

After convincing yourself that you can fix the problem, quickly move on to the third F—Forget. This is a time to remind yourself that "no one plays golf perfectly." "Everyone mis-hits a shot now and then." This type of self-talk can allow you to forget the problematic shot quickly and get ready to focus on the next shot as an opportunity.

The final F—Focus—encourages you to direct your attention to the next shot in a positive manner. Try to stay with your usual preshot routine and go through those motions with a sense of confidence and eagerness.

You can see how the 4-F Technique integrates other aspects of *React*. It helps downplay problematic shots and gives you something to do other than stew about the many challenges (frustrations) in golf. Our students have reacted well to this technique. It seems to help golfers at all levels of skill, from absolute beginners to touring professionals.

Scoring React

You earn a check under the React category if you follow all four React rules on the hole: use only positive verbal comments when describing your game or yourself, defend yourself against negative comments, keep your attributions positive, and use the 4-F Technique to cope and stay optimistic if needed.

Smart Golf Total Score

By tallying the totals for Preparation, Positive Focusing, and PAR (Plan, Apply, React), you can evaluate the quality of your mental game. The maximum Smart Golf score is 74: 2 for Preparation plus 18 for Positive Focusing plus 54—that is, 18 for each PAR component. The example of Dan's round at the Winnetka Golf Club (Figure 1.1) showed that his Preparation earned a 1, his Positive Focusing 17, and his PAR subtotals 13, 14, and 15. Dan's Smart Golf total = 60. Another way of evaluating a Smart Golf total is to divide it by the maximum possible score to yield a percentage (60/74 = 81 percent). An analysis of that 81 percent suggests Dan generally did a good job using Smart Golf. However, the Plan component could use a bit more attention, as could Preparation and to a lesser extent Apply and React.

Spend a few minutes after each round of golf to review your Smart Golf score:

- Which component was your most consistent?
- Which component was least consistent?
- How could you improve each component?
- Which holes were associated with your best Smart Golf scores?
- Which holes were your most problematic from a Smart Golf perspective?

You may find it very useful to keep a record of your Smart Golf scores along with the parallel golf scores. The following page (Table 1.1) shows an example of one useful record-keeping form. You can set goals for your Smart Golf scores just as you do for your golf scores. See how close you can get to 100 percent—and see how your enjoyment of the game and your scores improve when you get there.

You now have the tools to simplify and score your mental game. If you prepare effectively before a round of golf, focus positively on your good or better shots while you're playing, and use the PAR system, you should notice an immediate improvement in the quality of your golfing experience. Research on this approach shows some dramatic improvements in scores and attitudes.

Table 1.1
Golf Stroke and Smart Golf Scores

Date:	August 4, 1996
Course:	Winnetka
PAR/Course Rating/Slope:	71/70.9/125
Stroke Score (Front + Back = Total):	40 + 41 = 81
Smart Golf Score (Prep + Pos Foc + P + A + R = Total; Total ÷ 74 = percent):	1 + 17 + 13 + 14 + 15 = 60 ÷ 74 = 81 percent
Comments:	Good reactions; increase commitment to shots

Like anything new, it may seem somewhat complicated at first. You may find, for example, that it takes awhile to get used to self-monitoring the components of Smart Golf. It could seem awkward and time-consuming to record this information while you are playing. Please be assured that everyone who has given this system a reasonable chance has found that he or she becomes more efficient using it quite quickly. After one or two rounds, the concepts become clearer and the criteria for when to check off each element fit more comfortably into the scoring procedure. We hope you will give it a chance and benefit from more completely evaluating and understanding your mental game.

The remainder of the book provides detailed information about each of the five elements of Smart Golf.

You will learn a variety of approaches to master each of the elements. Regarding Preparation, for example, how do you prepare if you only have a few minutes before your tee time? We use additional examples, including experiences of our students and examples of research on these techniques, to help bring the concepts to life.

2

Preparation

A round of golf can begin twenty-four hours before the tee time. During those twenty-four hours you have the opportunity to eat well or poorly, rest well or poorly, warm up effectively or ineffectively, and focus on the upcoming round or just grip it and rip it. For people who view golf as a good walk, hopefully unspoiled, preparation may have relatively little effect on the quality of the golfing experience. If you wish to obtain the best possible score, however, preparation can affect your round of golf tremendously—perhaps as much as the quality of your shot game on that day.

This chapter reviews elements of effective preparation to help you maximize your performance and minimize your risk of injury. We will discuss how to warm up, the use of a swing orientation session, the value of focusing, and an abbreviated five-minute version of effective preparation.

🏌 Warm-Up Phase

How many golfers do you know who are over forty years old and have never had back problems? Back, shoulder, knee, and hip problems can derail promising careers among elite golfers and can interfere dramatically with the enjoyment of the game among recreational golfers. Unfortunately, the peculiar nature of the golf swing itself (all of that coiling and uncoiling) has the potential to cause such injuries. Swinging the golf club places tremendous pressure on the lower back, on the knees, and on other areas of the body. One way to combat these forces is to take the prospect of injury very seriously. If you do that, you will seek out potential preventive measures.

Stretching is one of the best ways to reduce your chances of hurting yourself on the golf course. Stretching immediately before a round of golf can improve the range of motion in your muscles and joints. This can dramatically reduce the risk of injury from overextending a muscle or a joint. You can also develop a smoother, more powerful swing much earlier in the round if you stretch before teeing off at the first hole. If your muscles and joints are tight, you will not be able to pivot smoothly—and that will make it difficult to generate your maximum clubhead speed. You can also improve your timing early in a round through stretching. Let's put it this way—a Titanium Moon Rock Driver probably yields smaller dividends for most golfers than a few minutes of stretching every day (particularly before playing a round of golf).

Stretching can improve flexibility best if you use a full stretching routine (ten to thirty minutes) every day. Most golfers will not put that kind of time into stretching and flexibility. However, even if you spend just a few minutes before beginning a round by stretching a few key muscle groups, you can decrease the likelihood of injury and improve the efficiency and smoothness of your golf swing. Here are a few guidelines and suggested stretches that you might consider using as part of your warm-up:

- Jog in place or walk around briskly for a few minutes before you begin your stretching routine. Stretching works best when muscles are at least a little bit warm.
- Stretch slowly and gently, stretching to the point where you feel some tension. This is called *static stretching,* and it allows the muscles to adapt themselves to the stretch safely.
- Hold the stretch for as long as it is not painful, ideally ten to thirty seconds.
- Repeat each stretching exercise at least twice, preferably three times.
- Avoid bouncing when doing any stretching exercise. Bouncing gets you into *ballistic stretching,* which can create microscopic tears

and other injuries—just what you are trying to prevent by doing the exercise.

- Work with a personal trainer at your local health club or with a physical therapist if you find it difficult to develop a stretching routine on your own. If you decide you need help, try to find someone whose education includes exercise physiology and certification from the American College of Sports Medicine.

The following specific stretches are particularly helpful for golfers:

Shoulder blade stretch. Slowly reach up and back with one of your arms as if to grab your shoulder blade. Use your other hand to extend the stretch by grasping your elbow and pulling it across the back of your body. After doing one arm like this and holding the stretch for ten to thirty seconds, do the other arm.

Towel shoulder stretch. Hold a rolled golf towel at both ends and slowly take it from the front of your body (direct extension from the front of your chest) over your head and as far behind your back as possible. Try to keep your arms straight throughout this stretch.

Corner shoulder stretch.
Use the corner of the room and place one hand on each side of the corner at about your shoulders' width apart. Slowly extend your upper body toward the corner while stretching the muscles of your upper back and shoulders.

Trunk twister with club. Begin this exercise with your feet shoulder-width apart and your arms extended on the head and handle of a golf club. Keep your heels flat on the floor and your toes straight ahead. Now very, very slowly twist the trunk of your body to the right as far as you can, then return to the starting position. Next, twist very slowly to the left. This is an especially important exercise for golfers because it prepares your body to make a full shoulder turn.

Lower back stretch. Lie on your back with your knees straight. Pull one knee to your chest slowly while grasping your leg just behind the knee. Return to the starting position and repeat the stretch with the other leg.

Hamstring bench stretch. Rest one heel on a bench and keep your knee as straight as possible. Reach forward for your toes very slowly and gently, keeping your head down as you reach forward. Do the same with the other leg.

Quad stretch. Use your right hand for balance by placing it on a wall, bench, or chair. Stand erect and keep your back straight. Then bend the right knee and lift the right foot directly behind your body. Do this by holding the toes of your right foot with your left hand. Pull up on the right leg until you feel a slight discomfort in the quadriceps muscle (upper front part of your thigh). Make sure that you keep your back straight. Repeat the exercise with the other leg.

Orientation Phase

After warming up, you are now ready to hit some balls. Some golf courses are set up so you have to begin with putting and chipping or with longer shots, others let you follow your own preference based on your experiences. The key is to check your time and budget it to meet your needs. Last-minute rushing may throw you off for the round.

The swing orientation phase is a time to get in touch with (or oriented to) your swing to see what you brought to the course today. It is not a time to work on your mechanics. It is not a practice session. Focus on your rhythm and timing.

Long Game Orientation

Before you take your first full swing at the ball, make a few continuous warm-up swings. In these swings, begin swinging slowly, and gradually increase your swing length, pivot, and pace. You may see some players swinging this type of warm-up with two or three clubs together. The extra weight helps stretch the specific muscles used in the swing. (Note: If you have any shoulder injuries, avoid the extra weight.)

There is no one way to use this orientation session

most efficiently. Your body will help you in this area. If you need more time to loosen up your swing, you may want to begin with the wedge and move up every couple of clubs until you get to your driver. Some golfers feel loose all the time and prefer to start with a 5-iron. Others may focus on the clubs they use most frequently on the course.

Regardless of the clubs you use, make sure that you pick out a specific target on the driving range and an intermediate target to use as a guidepost—don't just whack the balls in some general direction. Make sure you use your alignment as you hit balls. This may require special care because of the positioning of mats. Mats can be pointed in one direction and your specific target could be in a rather different location. For many golfers, it may work best to align to a specific target that is parallel to the mat's alignment. Rehearse a few shots with each club until you are reasonably comfortable with the way you are hitting the ball. Then you can change targets. After every few balls, step behind the ball to confirm your alignment. Remember: misalignment to an intermediate target by just a few degrees will result in missed greens or worse.

Your purpose here is to find out how your swing is working—*not* to improve it. You're about to play a round of golf. Your swing is going to stay pretty much the same, no matter what technique you work on for the few minutes before teeing off. Rather than wasting your time on a vain effort, use this orientation to gather information you can really use. You may discover, for example, that you are hitting your irons particularly well, but you are struggling a bit with your woods. This could translate into relying on irons more than on woods, particularly in the first few holes. You may also discover something about the flight of your shots. Perhaps your ball is curving a bit less or a bit more than usual on this particular day. Rather than trying to make an adjustment for the degree of curve on the range, why not consider going with what you've got at the moment and simply adjust your aim accordingly? In other words, use the mini-practice before a round for observation, not correction.

Short Game Orientation

More than 65 percent of the scoring comes from the short game, yet most golfers spend less than 10 percent of their practice (orientation) time on it. Try to focus your short game orientation on matching your feel with the speed of the greens. Both feel and speed of the greens vary greatly from day to day and even from hour to hour. In the morning, newly cut greens tend to be faster than in the afternoon when the grass has grown. If you play in the morning, you may be more relaxed and use less tension in your grip pressure than in the afternoon. Also, work on your distance control by varying shot length and targets.

Try to spend at least a few minutes putting and chipping, varying the shots that you hit. You're looking for feel in this part of your orientation. Start with very short putts and build up to longer putts. Be sure to include some thirty- to forty-foot lag putts to get a feel for speed. Meanwhile, make sure you follow the usual procedures of alignment and preshot routine. You can interfere with your sense of feel and confidence if you alter your routine substantially on the practice putting green.

Just as it's useful to vary the length and difficulty of your putts during your orientation, it helps to vary chipping in the same way. You would improve your sense of feel and confidence most by practicing some very simple chips and then moving on to more challenging ones. You can begin with rather short chips with 6- or 7-irons (run-up shots) and move on to pitching wedges and sand wedge flop shots. Since this is a mini-practice, you may only have a chance to hit a few different shots of these sorts. Aim primarily to go through a variety of chips to get a feel for the ball and your stroke at the moment.

Focus Phase

By this phase, you have stretched, warmed up, and hit a variety of shots, including putts and chips. Your next task is to focus on this round of golf. You may find it useful to ask yourself several key questions:

1. How will the weather affect play on the first few holes?
   - How brisk are the winds?
   - How variable are they?
   - Will the temperature have an impact on the ball?
2. What are the course conditions like today?
   - How wet or dry is the course?
   - What kind of condition are the greens in?
   - How has the grass been cut (at least on the first visible hole)?
3. Who am I playing with?
   - Is this going to be a competitive match or a friendly, casual game?
   - Are the other players easy to be around or are they challenging in some respect?
   - Am I playing with better players or weaker players than myself?
   - How will the relative skills of the players affect my anxiety level or my desire to play especially well?
4. How am I going to play the first hole?
   - What is my specific plan for my tee shot and for my other shots for that hole?

The answers to these questions can dramatically affect your approach to this particular round of golf. It helps to think these things out before teeing off on the first hole. That way, you can keep your focus on the feel of the shot and your specific targets. Otherwise, you may find it very distracting to suddenly discover, for example, that the ball isn't rolling out there today because the course is unusually wet. Or you may find yourself suddenly distracted by the extremely poor play or the extremely effective play of your partners.

Preparation: A Five-Minute Version

Here are some very common things that happen to people who want to break away for a round of golf:

- The phone rings and you simply can't get off the phone, despite squirming and strong eagerness to get the golf course.
- You suffer a golfer's delusion in estimating the amount of traffic you are likely to face between your point of origin and your course.
- You try to do "just one more thing" before you leave.
- You get halfway to the course and realize that it's much warmer than you thought—or much colder than you thought—so you need to get a change of clothes before teeing off.

- You leave your clubs or golf shoes in the garage—or your spouse's car.
- You lose track of the time and then you suddenly realize. . . .

One of our friends went beyond any of these scenarios. She was speeding to the course when she was pulled over by a police officer. As the officer fumbled around with the usual paperwork, checking to see that the car hadn't been stolen, our friend became increasingly anxious. She begged the officer, "OK, already! If you are going to give me a ticket, please make it quick, I have a tee time to make!" The officer obliged and wrote the fastest $75 speeding ticket in his life.

Various combinations of these scenarios can leave you with only a few minutes before you are due to tee off. What do you do then? You can either rush madly to the first tee and chat with your friends about what happened to you before getting there—or you can find some way to get yourself truly ready to play a round of golf.

A participant in one of our Smart Golf seminars, Don Peters, a medium-handicapper from Hinsdale, Illinois, observed that he performed better when he took the time to prepare fully—to go through what Walter Hagen used to call a "smooth-out routine." For Don, this included getting to the course early enough to hit a variety of shots at the driving range. He also took time to do some putting and chipping. He used the time as well to stretch and to focus on his round of golf. This focusing included reviewing the early holes and going over his plan for how to play those holes.

In comparing a few of his rounds during the seminar, Don indicated that his performance was notably off on the days that he rushed out on the first tee without his usual thirty-minute preparation routine. His best performances, in contrast, came when he had devoted the full amount of time he needed for preparation and focusing.

These observations led Don to a discovery that you can apply to your own game. Prior to one recent round, he did not have enough time to go through anything like his full half-hour routine. Instead, he found himself with less than five minutes before he had to hit his first shot. He decided to use this time to prepare himself as best he could rather than simply wait around the first tee and talk to his playing partners. Don stretched as much as he could (a couple of minutes is a fairly good amount of time to do some basic stretching). He also took a few swings and, while stretching and swinging, planned how he was going to play the first hole. In other words, he used his minutes, few as they were, as a window of opportunity to prepare as fully as he could. Normally, when he couldn't fit in his whole routine, he'd have skipped it entirely—chatting with his friends and then stepping up to hit the first shot without any preparation at all. This often led to a shaky feeling and to inconsistencies on the first few holes. The new approach helped him feel more relaxed and focused beginning with his very first swing.

The story of Don Peters shows one approach to abbreviated preparation. If you have literally just a few minutes, you can at least do some stretching and some mental preparation. You can consider some of the questions about weather and course conditions as you are stretching. You can also review your plan for the first hole and consider the nature of your playing partners or match while stretching.

If possible, you might have time to hit a ball or two with a 7- or 8-iron and rehearse a putt or chip or two. However, we strongly advise against hitting any balls or practicing any putts if you cannot do so with your usual preshot routine. It does you no good to rush out to a driving range and whack a couple of balls with a 7-iron if you don't have time to prepare mentally and physically for each shot. Use the following saying as a guideline: "Practice as you play; play as you practice." The same applies to putting. It won't help you at all to drop a ball or two on a putting green and walk up and just hit the ball toward the hole without going through your usual approach to putt it.

To summarize, here's the essence of the five-minute preparation:

1. *Stretch:* Keep it slow and focus on potentially troublesome areas such as shoulders and lower back.
2. *Focus:* Consider course and weather conditions, plan for the first hole, and consider the nature of your game or match.
3. *Mini-orientation:* Stroke a few chips, putts, and 7- or 8-irons—but only if you can use your full preshot routine for each shot. Otherwise, make some continuous swings, beginning slowly, just to warm up your muscles.

If you do not have time to complete the three aspects of this abbreviated preparation, at least do some stretching and focusing. Hitting actual golf balls takes the most time and yields the least payoff for the amount of time expended.

The Ill-Prepared Versus the Well-Prepared Golfer

Let's take a look at examples of how two levels of preparation can play out. See if these examples remind you of your own experiences, on both ends of the preparedness continuum.

Ill Prepared

Ned, a low-handicapper, scheduled a late afternoon Friday round with a few good friends. After he scheduled

Preparation

the round (a week in advance), he gave it very little thought. When Friday rolled around, he noticed the game on his calendar. He had a busy day looming ahead of him when he saw the golf outing. But the weather was very cooperative and he felt confident that he could get out to the course in time for a great start to the weekend.

As the time drew near for Ned to leave his office, he got an urgent call from a colleague. Ned was very involved in his real estate development business and was in the midst of several deals. His colleague called to tell him about a major problem that just emerged. Ned took the call and did some problem solving about obtaining alternative funding for a project about which he and his colleague were quite concerned. He became distracted during this problem-solving process. He lost track of time and before he knew it he was in deep trouble regarding his impending tee time. He made his excuses to his colleague, grabbed his briefcase, and blasted out of the office. He had to drive well beyond the speed limit, anxiously scanning the horizon for police cars.

Ned pulled into the parking lot of the golf course with two minutes to spare prior to the appointed tee time. He had already pulled off his street shoes during the drive; he quickly got his golf shoes on his feet, grabbed his clubs, and started running for the first tee. He got there just as his playing partners started walking down the first fairway. He called out to them and they waved back, laughing at his disheveled appearance. Ned had half his shirt out of his pants and he looked like a frazzled wreck. One of his friends called out, "Nice going Ned! Cutting it a little close today, aren't we?" Ned called back, "Just watch the fairway and you'll see my ball sailing over your heads in two seconds."

He excused himself to the group waiting to tee off and prepared for his first shot. He grabbed the first ball and the first tee he could find and his driver. He neglected to consider the fact that this hole was a par 5, unreachable for him. The wind was in his face and the driver offered no advantage relative to a lesser club that he could hit more consistently down the middle. Nonetheless, he quickly plunked his tee into the ground, stepped back for a moment to survey his projected shot. He stepped up to the ball, waggled briefly, and proceeded to dribble the ball into a pond thirty feet in front of him.

He quickly ran back to his golf bag, grabbed another ball, placed it on the tee and managed to hit a rather wicked slice into some trees on the right side of the fairway. He again made his apologies to the group standing around the tee, who were chuckling through their irritation at the delay, and ran out to meet his playing partners. When he caught up to his partners one of his friends said, in half-consoling tones, "Well, Ned, I've never seen you hit two such sorry-looking shots in a row in my life!" "Yeah, yeah," responded a less than enthused Ned.

This true story shows what poor preparation can do even to a low-handicapper like Ned. His friend's remark about never having seen Ned hit "two such sorry-looking shots in a row" was accurate. Those two shots were purely a reflection of Ned's inability to focus and to take a slow, smooth backswing. If such shots happened during the middle of the round, that would be one thing. It creates a different feeling for the game if the first shot of the round is so uncharacteristically troublesome. This is why preparation is so critical.

Well Prepared

Ann, like Ned, scheduled a Friday afternoon round of golf. Unlike Ned, however, Ann had thought quite a bit about this round prior to the actual day. She was looking forward to playing it and saw it as a highlight of her week. The day of the round, Ann brought her putter up to her office and practiced putting between appointments and phone calls. Ann, an attorney in downtown Chicago, had plenty of work on her desk and many issues to tackle during her work week. However, she made a firm commitment to herself to play that Friday afternoon round of golf. She would not let anything interfere with that plan—as soon as she saw that the weather was going to cooperate.

Ann got to the golf course forty-five minutes before the round was scheduled to begin. After checking in with the starter, she got half a bucket of balls and took them to the driving range. After a reasonably thorough stretching routine, she took her 7-iron and found a target on the driving range. She hit very easy shots in the early phase of her warm-up. She hit the 7-iron, went down to a few pitching wedges, then up to some 5-irons, and finally finished with some 3-woods and drivers. She left a few balls in her bucket for some additional shots if she had time after putting.

She selected her putter and a couple of chipping clubs and went to the practice green. She worked on her putting for awhile, starting with simple short putts and building up to long lag putts. She followed a similar routine for her chipping. Ann ended the mini-practice with a couple of lob wedges of twenty feet or so.

She still had a few minutes left, but decided against hitting any additional balls. She felt she knew what her swings were like that day and wanted to concentrate on the round she was about to play. She went over to the first hole and surveyed the situation. She realized that a sizable rain the night before had left the course wet. She also noticed there was little breeze to consider. She thought about her playing partners and the type of round she was about to experience. Ann anticipated a very friendly, casual game with minimal emphasis on competition. As a medium-handicapper, she was probably the second-best player in the group. Two of the other players were high-handicappers. She decided that they would probably play a very low-cost team bet that would be fun, add a little spice to the round, but not make it very distracting or pressure-packed.

Ann reviewed her plan for the first hole, including the tee shot and likely follow-up shots. She considered the flag position in this calculation. She felt reasonably confident and eager to play.

Ann purposely went down a club for the tee shot on the first hole. Instead of hitting a 3-wood (which she would do if she felt brimful of confidence), she hit a 5-wood. She decided to "play for confidence, not for score" in the early part of the round. She hit a mediocre shot off the tee but was in the fairway, albeit further back than desired. She again hit conservative follow-up shots and completed the first hole (the number 8 handicap hole) with a perfectly satisfactory bogey.

Ill Prepared Versus Well Prepared

You can see the rather dramatic contrast between Ann, the well-prepared golfer, and Ned, the ill-prepared golfer. You may have noticed the difference in tension levels and sense of purpose in their initial preparations. Ann oriented herself to an enjoyable and relaxing round of golf. Ned failed to do that and found himself anxious before the round and quite disturbed by his initial shots.

Golf has a way of accentuating feeling states: a negative feeling can get even more negative during a round of golf and a positive feeling can get even more positive. On the other hand, the distracting and involving nature of a round of golf can take an anxious or confused state and transform it into a pleasant, obsessive haze that is a very satisfying part of the game. Certainly, that is the way A. J. Balfour viewed it in 1890, as the quote in the next paragraph indicates. Yet if you begin the round in a more positive state, you are more likely to enjoy it from the first precious moment you step on the course. A well-prepared, positive outlook can maximize your chances of starting well and continuing that way.

> A tolerable day, a tolerable green, a tolerable opponent, supply, or ought to supply, all that any reasonably constituted human being should require in the way of entertainment. With a fine, sea view, and a clear course in front of him, the golfer should find no difficulty in dismissing all worries from his mind, and regarding golf, even if it be indifferent golf, as the true and adequate end of man's existence. . . . No inconvenient reminiscences of the ordinary workaday world, no intervals of weariness or monotony interrupt the pleasures of the game. And of what other recreation can this be said? [Wind, 1954]

This chapter encouraged you to take preparation seriously so as to get the most from your capabilities as a golfer and to reduce your risk of injuries from playing this game. Perhaps it would help to think of golf requiring four and a half hours to play: four hours for the golf and half an hour for preparation. Effective preparation includes a warm-up phase (with stretching and orientation to your swing and feel for that day) and a focus phase. It's possible to use a few minutes, if that's all you have, to complete a very abbreviated version of this preparation.

The next chapter, Positive Focusing, describes a technique that can keep you focused on the positive aspects of golf, while keeping the inevitable problems in perspective. Tobias Smollett suggested in 1771 that golf "must without all doubt keep the appetite on edge and steel the constitution against all common attacks of distemper" (Wind, 1954). Positive focusing may not help your golf game provide all these benefits, but it should keep your focus sharper and help you enjoy yourself more.

3

Positive Focusing

 Imagine that you're a relatively inexperienced high-handicapper. You're playing in a competitive match with one of your friends against two other people you don't know very well. By the twelfth hole, you figure your partner's back must be hurting from carrying you almost the whole round thus far.

You hit your best tee shot of the day on this hole. Remarkably, you follow that shot with an excellent 5-iron to nine feet below the hole. Your partner runs over to high-five you; both of you are feeling no pain at this point. You practically run to the green, feeling your heart pounding along the way.

You mark your ball and survey the putt as your partner and the people on the opposing team hit their lag putts. Your putt looks like it has a slight right-to-left break uphill. You're telling yourself, "You can handle this putt—no problem." You see yourself making the birdie and excitedly winning the hole for your team. You go through your preshot routine a little faster than usual. But you're excited and ready to knock that ball in the center of the cup. Unfortunately, in your eagerness to make the glorious bird, remembering the dictum "Never up, never in," you misread the speed and knock the putt three and a half feet above the hole. You rather quickly hit it again—remembering the dictum "Miss 'em quick." Your three-and-a-half-footer for par slides by the left edge. Your bogey costs your team the hole.

What's your reaction? While standing on the next tee, are you thinking about the three putt or the great tee shot and 5-iron shot?

Most golfers say they would find themselves angrily musing about the three putt. When performing any difficult task, people tend to focus on their mistakes. Golf is no exception. These images often haunt golfers, blocking the memory of excellent shots—even those hit on the very same hole. We tend to magnify our errors or bad shots; we tend to minimize our better shots. Yet if you focus on your triumphs, not your tragedies, you will perform much better.

A technique that provides an antidote to this overemphasis on bad shots is *positive focusing*. Positive focusing is thinking about and recalling your better shots while trying to ignore your poorer shots as you play golf. This technique accepts the fact people often view a half-full glass of water as half-empty. Golfers have choices about how to direct their attention during a round of golf. If you direct your attention to the positive aspects of what you are doing—positively focus—you will perform better than if you direct your attention to problems in your swing or the misfortunes that inevitably occur while playing golf. In this chapter, we show you how to use positive focusing, describe why it works, and emphasize its importance by reviewing some of our research on its effectiveness in golf.

How to Use Positive Focusing

A tennis player just misses the white line marking the boundary of the court. She almost hit a great shot. Two inches over and that ball would have been a winner. A bowler almost throws a strike, but instead leaves one pin standing. That bowler almost threw a perfect strike. Missed shots in golf, on the other hand, have far more drama to them. A slice into the top of the trees 200 yards away looks much uglier than a mis-hit tennis shot or a missed pin in bowling. Think about some of your misses in golf. You may recall some worm burners or shots that you hooked into a watery grave. No other sport displays problems so dramatically and publicly.

You can't simply tell yourself "think more positively" to manage the spectacle of some of those missed shots. More powerful medicine is required. Positive focusing helps you take several specific steps to get your attention away from the problems and, instead, sharply tuned in to what you are doing well. Here are the four steps of positive focusing: identify good or better shots, record good or better shots, replay good or better shots, and forget less than good shots.

Identify good or better shots. After each hole, while you are standing on the tee to the next hole and before you hit your next tee shot, identify each shot on the previous hole that you hit reasonably well. These are shots that you consider good, very good, or excellent compared to your usual shots. Of course, the definition of a good or better shot can vary depending on your skill and experience level. For a beginner, anything that gets in the air and moves in a generally forward direction could very legitimately meet the good or better criteria. A touring professional, in contrast, would list many other elements among the criteria for a good or better shot. These elements would include trajectory, distance, and accuracy. We strongly encourage you to pick a lenient standard when using this technique. This means that most golfers should find at least one shot on almost every hole that they can identify in the good or better range.

Record good or better shots. Under your name on the scorecard put the term "Pos Foc" or just "PF." Use this PF for the line under your name instead of writing in the name of a fellow player. Then, after each hole, write in each shot that you executed on that hole that met your good or better criteria. Figure 3.1 shows an example that you might find useful.

In this example, Bill, a medium-handicapper, played the White tees at the Winnetka Golf Club. This is the same course that was used for the example in Chapter One. Note that in this case, Bill recorded something under his "Pos Foc" for every hole. In some cases, for example, Holes #3, #6, and #14, Bill only recorded one entry. Other cases included two entries; one (#12) had three entries. Bill earned the three entries on the twelfth hole with a birdie.

Here are some more abbreviations that our students have found useful when using this technique:

- *Woods:* D = Driver; 2W–9W = 2-wood to 9-wood.
- *Irons:* 1–9 = 1- to 9-irons.
- *Chips:* Club + C; 5C–PWC = 5-iron chip to pitching wedge chip.
- *Bunker Shots:* SB = sand wedge from bunker; SW = sand wedge not from bunker.
- *Putts:* LP = Long Putt (ten feet and longer); P = five- to nine-foot putt; SP = Short Putt (four feet or less).

Replay good or better shots. Take a few seconds while waiting to tee off on the subsequent hole to recreate each shot that you recorded as meeting your good

Figure 3.1
Positive Focusing: A Scorecard Example

HOLE NUMBER	1	2	3	4	5	6	7	8	9	OUT
Blue Tees	349	519	157	419	362	413	167	372	407	3165
White Tees	336	501	144	504	346	396	134	361	397	3020
Par	4	5	3	4	4	4	3	4	4	35
Handicap	13	1	15	5	9	7	17	11	3	
Bill	4	6	3	5	5	5	4	6	5	43
Pos Foc	3W 8	5W 8	LP	5W 3W	3W LP	SB D	LP	PW	7	

HOLE NUMBER	10	11	12	13	14	15	16	17	18	IN	TOT	HCP	NET
Blue Tees	527	386	305	192	346	480	387	221	443	3287	6452		
White Tees	511	378	294	163	330	472	372	209	436	3165	6185		
Par	5	4	4	3	4	5	4	3	4	36	71		
Handicap	2	8	18	16	14	6	12	10	4				
Bill	6	5	3	4	4	5	5	4	5	41	84		
Pos Foc	3W	7	PW 3W	9C	P	LP 6	5W	7C	PW				

or better criteria from the previous hole. You can create a visual image that includes the shot as it looked immediately after hitting it. Or you can create an image of how the swing felt and what the ball felt like coming off the clubface. You can begin the image from the planning phase leading to club selection and then to set-up. Or you can begin it from the execution phase, starting with the take-away from the ball.

Try to remember as much as you can about each of your good or better shots. Try to remember what it felt like to plan the shot, to set up for it, to execute the swing, and to hit the ball. If you tend to be visually oriented, you will be able to recall the ball in flight and how it landed. More feel-oriented golfers may remember what it felt like to swing the club and make solid contact with the ball while executing the stroke. Try to use as much detail as you can in these images. For example, can you recall how confident you felt when you selected the club and the shot? Can you recall the grip pressure as you were executing the swing? Can you identify a sense of satisfaction as you felt the clubhead hitting the ball? Can you recall a sense of excitement as the ball landed on or near your specific target?

As you get used to using this aspect of positive focusing, these replays should take literally just a few seconds each. If you had a particularly good hole and you are slated to tee off as soon as you get to the next tee, you may find it useful to replay at least one of your good or better shots on your way to the tee. This phase of Smart Golf should not slow down play. It is simply meant as a device to channel your attention to what you are doing well as you play. Many golfers spend time talking to themselves or their playing partners about problematic shots after each hole. Instead of that, positive focusing redirects you to concentrate on what you did well on the previous hole.

Forget less than good shots. You can remember your problematic shots and use them as guidance for subsequent practice and instruction—after the round. You can remind yourself that no one plays perfect golf. You can also try to think of problematic shots as opportunities to recover and to try shots that could be interesting. You can remind yourself that additional practice and instruction can improve the quality of your golf swing, its efficiency, and your ability to use it on the course. You can only play with what you brought to the course on that day. Improvement must wait for another time and another setting. Why not try to enjoy yourself and get the most out of your time on the golf course?

Positive Focusing in Action

Bill's round and his positive focus during it in Figure 3.1 provide a useful example of all four elements of this technique.

You can see on the first hole that Bill was pleased with both his 3-wood tee shot and his 8-iron approach shot to the green. Note that the handicap for the hole is 13. Bill played to an 18 handicap from the White tees that day at the Winnetka Golf Club. This means that the first hole is a stroke hole for Bill. His handicap suggests that a personal par of 5 would be reasonable. Also, since the first hole also produces an unusual share of jitters for most people, including Bill, this performance on Hole #1 was particularly gratifying.

After the hole, while he was waiting for his turn on the second tee, Bill recalled as much as he could about those two shots. He remembered selecting a 3-wood for the tee shot, partly because the wind was in the golfers' faces at that point. He wanted to have a chance to hit the ball far enough into the wind to have a relatively short shot into the heavily guarded small green. He remembered committing to the 3-wood before beginning his preshot routine. Bill then reminded himself to grip the club lightly to avoid overswinging in response to the tension of the first tee. He remembered the feeling of taking a nice, smooth take-away and thinking about his target as he swung. He felt in balance after swinging and recalled the pleasant sensation and the loud click made by the club hitting through the ball when he made solid contact before the ball took off toward the target. He could see in his mind's eye the ball fading in a medium-high trajectory toward the target in the fairway.

He also remembered a similar commitment to his 8-iron second shot. The execution of the swing went as well as the tee shot. The ball landed on the widest part of the green on the right side and stayed there. As he was waiting for his turn on the second tee, he replayed this shot and could see it land on the green again. He enjoyed remembering the feeling of making solid contact with the ball and having the swing feel easy and in balance.

Bill's play of the sixteenth hole provides another good example of positive focusing. Despite the sixteenth hole's 12 handicap rating, it is definitely among the easier holes on the golf course. It is a relatively straightforward par 4 of moderate length. Bill mis-hit his tee shot on the hole. He popped it up quite short. He recalled working hard to come up with a conservative plan for hitting his second shot after he mis-hit his first shot so dramatically. He tried thinking about his plan for the rest of the hole as a way of ignoring the popped-up tee shot. He realized that the green was only in his reach if he hit the best 3-wood of his life. He felt much more confident hitting a 5-wood and then leaving himself with an easy pitch or chip onto the green.

Bill recalled hitting his 5-wood second shot as he intended and enjoyed watching its gentle fade toward the specific target that he selected. The remainder of the hole was OK. His chipping and putting did not meet his good or better criteria on that hole. Yet the 5-wood gave him something positive to think about as he prepared to hit his tee shot on the long and difficult par 3 seventeenth hole.

Clearly, positive focusing keeps the golfer's mind preoccupied with positive outcomes. Let's consider why that can prove so useful.

Why Does Positive Focusing Improve Performance?

The best way to understand how and why positive focusing improves performance is to try the technique yourself. After you try it even for one round of golf, you will have a much better idea of the changes that the technique can induce in you.

Research on this approach and our own experience teaching it to serious students of golf have helped us understand it. Figure 3.2 shows four dimensions that are affected by positive focusing: positive mood, optimism, attention control, and coping. As you read the story that follows, see if you can identify the effects of positive focusing on each of these dimensions.

Larry Zelikoff is a trader by profession at the Chicago Board Options Exchange. He is a very numbers-oriented and results-oriented person. He also sets high standards for himself in all aspects of his life. Larry has been a competitive athlete in a number of sports. He demonstrates his competitive intensity in golf by

Figure 3.2
Four Benefits of Positive Focusing

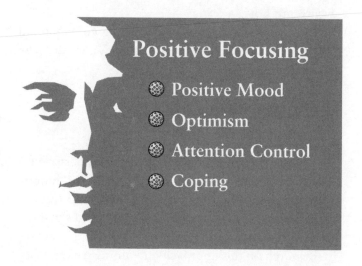

working hard at his game and achieving a very low handicap (2 to 5). Unfortunately, Larry's competitive intensity has created a rather turbulent style of playing the game.

Larry and his wife sometimes take lessons together with DeDe Owens. One day, his wife whispered to DeDe before a lesson, "Oh, you've got to help him, DeDe! He's been in a really bad mood lately!" She spoke in a joking manner, but she was genuinely concerned about the way her husband tortured himself on the golf course. Almost any shot that was less than perfect was greeted with a series of angry mutterings, at best. A frown became permanently etched on his face during some of his rounds of golf. This seemed especially ironic considering that Larry's skill level put him in the upper 3 percent of the golfing population.

DeDe introduced Larry to positive focusing. The first week that Larry began using the new approach, he played five rounds of golf. He reported an amazing transformation. "My wife and my regular playing partners didn't know who I was! They thought that someone had taken over my body or that I had drunk some magic potion!"

Larry reported that from the moment he started using the system, the anger and negativity that had become his personal trademark on the golf course disappeared. He amazed himself: "I know that this is hard to believe, but I didn't really even feel angry inside when I was mis-hitting shots. And believe me, I had opportunities to get pretty angry. I even shot an 87 during the week. This would usually be a total disaster for me. People wouldn't want to be around me for many hours after a round like that. Yet, I was able to take it one shot at a time. I treated each shot as its own challenge and stayed focused on what I was trying to do. I have absolutely never had an experience like that in my life. When I hit a bad shot, I just went after the ball thinking, 'OK, let's see how you can get back in play on this shot.' Or I would get into a challenging situation and just see it for that and think of it as part of the game.

"I had one hole on which I hit a perfect tee shot and found it in this huge divot. It was a very fresh divot. Normally, I would be cursing the guy in the group ahead who failed to repair the divot. This time I thought, 'OK, I'll just take this 3-wood out and knock it up there toward the green.' I figured I could get it somewhere close to the green and maybe scramble home for par.

"This total transformation in attitude has made the game far more enjoyable. This is from someone who has been playing the game for more than twenty years!"

You can see that Larry developed a far more *positive mood* as a result of using positive focusing and other aspects of the Smart Golf approach. His reaction to his shot landing in the divot also reflected a certain *optimism* about the outcome of his efforts. His *attention* seemed focused on the present and the task at hand, rather than on extraneous matters such as the carelessness of the players in front of him or the problems that his sometimes errant shots created. He had obviously found a new way to *cope* with the challenges that golf presents to even highly skilled players.

Positive focusing's advantages for mood, optimism, attention, and coping seem convincing. In the next section, we review the results of research to show that these benefits play out rather nicely on the golf course.

Effectiveness of Positive Focusing in Golf

We believe that positive focusing is such an important aspect of the mental game that we want to prove to you, beyond a shadow of a doubt, that you will benefit from using this technique. To do that, we present the results of two studies that used this technique with golfers. When this technique was used with other athletes, such as figure skaters, swimmers, and bowlers, the athletes substantially improved their efforts and outcomes. As you will see, research with university-level golfers (very low-handicappers) and beginning golfers shows equal and substantial benefits from positive focusing.

Positive Focusing by University Golfers

Dan Kirschenbaum and Ron Bale had golfers (average handicap = 1) from the University of Cincinnati use a positive focusing technique very much like the one we advocate in our Smart Golf system. The golfers used positive focusing after each hole for ten competitive rounds. These golfers wrote down each shot that was good or better following every hole. After writing down

the good or better shots, the golfers were advised to recall everything that they could about those shots. For
example, they remembered how they positioned their
feet, the feel of the swings, and their target selections. If
possible, they actually pictured what the ball looked
like coming off the club and mentally watched its flight
until it reached its final landing position. This review
of the positive shots may be just as important as actually recording the shots that were good or better.

Figure 3.3 shows some of the effects of this approach. The figure shows that one participant in this
study (the one labeled "experimental") was the only
one of the five starters to improve his performance from
the beginning of the season to the end of the season.
This player went on to win the City of Cincinnati Championship two years later. He reported that the positive
focusing technique was "very helpful," and he said, "I
think for the first time that I can remember, this approach sets forth a method to help improve the mental
side of golf—and it's about time. This program could
do more for the average golfer than five lessons from a
professional."

The University of Cincinnati golf coach involved
with this research became so enthused about the results
of this initial study that he used the availability of this
mental skills training program as a recruitment device
in the following year. In the first year of implementing

the program, only a few of the freshmen were interested in participating. With the coach's enthusiasm behind us, every man on the team wanted to participate in the second year. We again found that participants improved their performances in competition after they learned the approach. Each participant also reported feeling better about his game and generally more positive on the golf course.

Figure 3.3
Positive Focusing Improved Performance
by a University Golfer

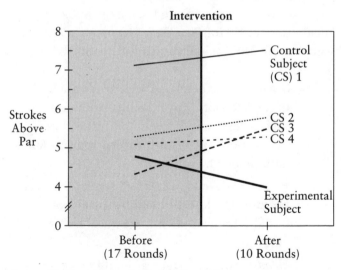

Source: Kirschenbaum and Bale (1980), p. 338.

Positive Focusing with Beginning Golfers

With another colleague of ours, Elizabeth Johnston-O'Connor, we completed a more elaborate test of the value of positive focusing for golfers in 1986. In that study, 109 beginning golfers took a series of lessons. The average handicap of these golfers was approximately 30. One of the purposes of this study was to see if the results obtained with expert university-level golfers could apply to novices.

Each of these beginning golfers received a pamphlet describing five key aspects of the golf swing. This pamphlet included fourteen illustrations of successive movements of the golf swing from the classic book by Jack Nicklaus entitled *Golf My Way*. The major points presented about Nicklaus's five swing elements were:

1. *Stance:* Position the ball just inside the heel of the left foot. Move the right foot closer for each successively lower club (9-iron closer than 8-iron, and so on). Extend arms to full natural length.

2. *Posture:* Strive for a relaxed, stable, balanced posture. The knees should be somewhat flexed, shoulders slightly forward, and back fairly straight.

3. *Head Position:* The head should be kept still from address to impact, almost as if the head

and neck were parts of a central axis around which the rest of the body turns.

4. *Downswing Initiation:* Lead with the feet by shifting weight toward the target. In succession following the feet, the ankles, knees, and then hips should move sideways toward the target.

5. *Follow-Through:* Hit *through* the ball, not *to* it by shifting weight to the left foot and letting the arms swing out and all the way up with continued acceleration.

All participants in the study attempted to hit whiffle golf balls three times in each of three sessions. The sessions were held once a week for three weeks.

The participants were divided into three groups. Each group observed their swings on videotape. The *positive self-monitoring* (or positive focusing) group completed a grid that included the five elements of the swing with spaces underneath each of them. They put pluses (+) under components executed well. The *neutral self-monitoring* group followed a parallel procedure to complete their grids. Their instructions were "each time that you can specifically identify how you executed one or more swing element, put a slash (/) in the table below, beside the swing number under the element." In other words, positive self-monitors recorded instances in which they executed components *well*; neutral self-monitors simply recorded *any* example of the elements of the swing. The *no self-monitoring* (or control) group simply observed themselves on videotape without further instructions.

Figure 3.4 shows changes in the quality of the golf swings for each of the three groups. Quality of golf swing in this research was measured by having trained observers record nine different elements of the golf swings as they appeared on videotape. Note that the

Figure 3.4
Positive Self-Monitoring (SM) Improved Quality of Golf Swings by Novice Golfers

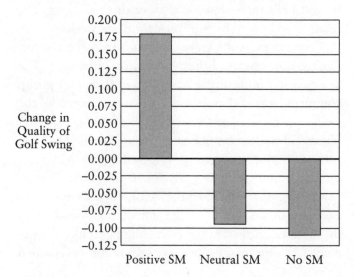

positive self-monitoring group improved the quality of their golf swings. Both the neutral self-monitoring and the no self-monitoring groups got worse in the course of the study.

Consistency of the golf swings also changed most dramatically for those who positively self-monitored. In other words, positive focusing helped narrow the range of the quality of their swings. The worst shots of the positive self-monitors became more similar to their best shots. The neutral and no-monitoring participants' best shots remained far better than their worst shots. Positive focusers also reported greater enjoyment and less difficulty with golf than participants in the other groups.

These studies show that with both elite and beginning golfers, it helps to focus very specifically on the more positive aspects of playing. Keeping track of what you do in a positive way may keep your confidence high enough to improve your concentration. Beginners, especially, may find looking at videotapes of themselves very disheartening. The beginning golfers that we video-taped really looked very awkward when attempting to hit the whiffle ball. In fact, quite often, they missed the ball entirely and practically fell over as they swung! If you observed yourself doing that on videotape, you, too, might feel very discouraged. Positive focusing counters that discouragement. It replaces discouragement with encouragement.

For elite players, relatively small errors can seem like dramatic goof-ups. We have played with dozens of professional golfers and noticed this occurring regularly. A shot most golfers would consider very good, they would view as poor. As performance improves, standards get more and more stringent. Still, players at all skill levels can find aspects of their performance that meet reasonable "good or better" standards.

Positive focusing gives you something to do to draw your attention away from the sometimes dramatically negative events that occur on the golf course. Each of the four elements of the technique, from identifying good or better shots to recording those shots on your scorecard to replaying those shots to forgetting the problematic shots, plays an important part in its effectiveness. Positive focusing can affect your mood, your attitude, your attention, and your ability to cope on the golf course. These effects can improve the quality and consistency of your golf swings.

You may recognize the advantages of positive focusing in other aspects of your life beyond golf. You can use this approach to handle crises, to deal with tragedy in your life, and for other challenges. Many wise individuals have observed these effects over the centuries. Yet few people manage to use this approach systematically on the golf course on a regular basis. Perhaps you will find further support for the wisdom of this method in the following observations:

> People are disturbed not by things, but by the view which they take of them.
>
> Epictetus, first century, *The Encheiridion*

> There is nothing either good or bad, but thinking makes it so.
>
> William Shakespeare, seventeenth century, *Hamlet*

> A person's behavior springs from his ideas. . . . It is his attitude toward life which determines his relationship to the outside world.
>
> Alfred Adler, twentieth century, *Social Interests: Challenge to Mankind*

4

Plan

Do you play golf to challenge yourself? To enjoy the thrill of hitting the occasional wonderful shot? To enjoy the company of your friends? To get a mental or physical reprieve from your everyday life? To exercise?

Most golfers answer these questions with "Yes, all of the above!" Golf's ability to fulfill these many purposes has made it the most popular sport in the world. Yet sometimes a combination of these reasons for playing can prove very distracting. You can focus on the social aspect of the game, listening or telling a good story, and find yourself failing to pay attention to the demands of your next shot. Heated arguments about competition or wagers can also keep you from identifying your specific target or taking care to ensure appropriate alignment during your preshot routine.

Fortunately, golf only requires a series of brief intervals—thirty-five to forty seconds apiece—to execute your shots, with many minutes between shots. If you think of it this way and learn how to focus when you approach your ball, you can see that plenty of time remains for the other purposes of the game.

This chapter can help you use some of those brief intervals to plan your approach to each hole. If you understand the principles reviewed in this chapter, planning need not become a burden or take more than a minute per hole. When you develop an effective plan you decrease your anxiety. The plan helps you anticipate what could and will happen on the hole. It provides strategies to handle any situation. This should lower the fear of the unknown on the hole, increase your sense of confidence and purpose, and result in lowered scores and more enjoyment.

You can get the most out of your plan when you understand some critical factors that affect the process of planning. First, we invite you to analyze your current skill level objectively. You can develop a truly effective plan only if you understand what your current skills allow you to do on the golf course.

Second, we help you understand why golfers have such difficulties planning effectively. These difficulties affect all of us. The psychology of planning takes some surprising turns. We will review some fascinating research on this topic so you can see for yourself how common distortions in thinking can wreak havoc with your logic on the links.

To overcome these psychological pitfalls, we offer a system of planning that begins with establishing your personal par for each hole. Our approach uses three other planning principles to help you work out ways to achieve that personal par: conservation, wide first, and safety first. We will describe how to use all four of these planning principles in this chapter.

Finally, we show you how to use this approach by asking you to develop your own hypothetical plans to play four holes on one of the best golf courses in the United States, Dubsdread—the course on which the PGA Tour contests the Motorola Western Open each summer. We provide examples of plans for four golfers to play those holes. You can compare your hypothetical plans to these examples to improve your ability to use Smart Golf.

Assessment of Current Golf Skills

You can construct a meaningful plan only when you have a reasonably clear understanding of your golf skills. We assume you already know your handicap. If you do not know your handicap, please consult with your local club professional to determine it. Almost every golf club in the United States has a means for maintaining an accurate handicap. The handicap provides a good indication of overall skill level. Handicaps allow golfers of widely divergent skills to compete on approximately equal levels.

Knowing your handicap does not help you understand which specific golf skills you execute better than others, however. For example, quite a few golfers in their sixties maintain relatively low handicaps. Many of these senior golfers have excellent short games and can hit the ball in a reliable direction with a wide variety of clubs. Younger golfers with similar handicaps may get there by hitting much longer tee shots and relying on their long games to compensate for less than precise short games.

What are your strengths and weaknesses as a golfer? To add considerable detail to your answer to this important question, we constructed an assessment form for your use. Take a look at the following material now to get an idea of the range of golf skills that we believe are critical to develop a maximally helpful game plan. Read over the instructions and the notes, then see if you can figure out how well Pat—the student who filled out the form—is doing.

**Assessment of Golf Skills:
Strengths and Weaknesses**

Name: _____Pat_____

Date: _____7/1/97_____

Handicap: _24_____

Instructions: To indicate a strength, place a plus (+) under each golf skill if you currently execute that skill at the level specified by the criterion *most of the time.* (Trajectory control skills require correct executions 67 percent or more of the time). To indicate a weakness, place a minus (–) if you do *not* execute that skill at the criterion most of the time. If you are not sure of your current skill level, enter a question mark(?). Enter *NA* for "Not Applicable" if a skill does not apply to you (for example, if you do not use 2- or 3-irons, enter *NA* for questions about them).

Distance and Direction

	Distance[1]	*Direction*[2]
Woods	$C^3 = \pm 10$ yards	$C = L/R$ 10 yards
Driver	–	–
3	–	–
4 or 5	+	+
7 and others	NA	NA
Irons	$C = \pm 10$ yards	$C = L/R$ 10 yards
2–3	–	–
4–6	–	–
7–9	+	+
Pitching (yards)	$C = \pm 20$ yards	$C = L/R$ 20 yards
80–95	–	–
65–79	–	–
50–64	+	–
35–49	+	+
20–34	+	+

Chipping (yards)	C = ± 10 feet	C = L/R 10 yards
30+	–	–
20–29	+	–
10–19	+	+
<10	+	+

Putting (yards)	C = ± 2 feet	C = L/R 2 feet
30+	–	–
20–29	+	–
10–19	+	+
<10	+	+

Sands (yards)	C = ± 10 feet	C = L/R 10 feet
12+	–	–
16–24	–	–
10–15	+	+
<9	+	+

Usual Trajectory

C = 50% or more of the time

	Height			Curvature		
	Low	Medium	High	L to R	Straight	R to L
Driver		+			?	
Fairway Woods		+			?	
Long Irons (2–3)	+				?	
Middle Irons (4–6)		+		?	+	
Short Irons (7–9)			+		+	

Trajectory Control

C = 67% of Attempts[4]

	Height			Curvature		
	Low	Medium	High	L to R	Straight	R to L
Driver		+		+		
Fairway Woods		+				
Long Irons (2–3)	+			+		
Middle Irons (4–6)		+		+	+	
Short Irons (7–9)		+			+	

Notes:

[1]Distance = Criterion measured using a vertical line from directly above (+) to directly below (–) the specific target, regardless of the direction (position to the left or right of the hole).

[2]Direction = Criterion measured using a horizontal line from the left to the right of the specific target, regardless of distance (position above or below the hole).

[3]C = Criterion for determining whether your current execution of that skill qualifies as a current strength in your game.

[4]Attempt = Deliberate attempts to manipulate the trajectory of the ball.

Pat is an avid player who maintains a 24 handicap. A review of the form shows that Pat has generally better control of his shorter clubs. He can predict the distance and direction of his 5-wood and his shorter irons with greater confidence than he can predict the distance or direction of his driver, 3-wood, and long- and mid-irons. He also showed less confidence in his longer wedge shots, longer chips, longer putts, and longer sand bunker shots. Pat indicated that his usual trajectory included medium height and basically straight middle and short irons. He showed some doubt about the predictability of the curvature of most of his shots, as well. Finally, Pat indicated a much better ability to control the trajectory of his shots when he was attempting to hit them left to right than when he was attempting to hit them higher than normal or from right to left.

You can see that this level of assessment allows Pat to predict what club to use when he absolutely has to hit a shot straight. He could go to a 5-wood for relatively long shots that must go straight; he could hit a shorter iron to control both distance and direction.

Armed with this level of understanding of his game, Pat can give clear direction to the parts of his game he works on in practice. Pat can also establish his plans to take advantage of his strengths while minimizing his weaknesses. For example, Pat would not want to put himself in a position where he had to hit a shot right to left or to hit one particularly high. On the other hand, he could do rather well from positions where he had to hit shots left to right or keep them low. This information should dramatically affect Pat's selection of specific targets and his understanding of his safest bail-out areas.

Can you complete a version of the form for yourself? You can modify the criteria to reflect your own skill level. Use more stringent criteria if you play to a low handicap (for example, you may want to count only putts holed out, not the ones where you get within two feet) and less stringent criteria if you currently play to a high handicap (for example, you may be doing very well to get putts within three feet instead of two feet). Can you identify your strengths and weaknesses at this level of specificity? If not, you are going to have greater difficulty using the planning strategies provided in the rest of this chapter.

It may also help to complete an assessment of this type before taking lessons from a teaching professional. You can bring this information to the lesson to better inform the teaching professional and provide useful direction to your work together. You can also revisit this assessment periodically. As your skills develop, you could modify your criteria (making them more stringent over time) and you could begin to track information in areas where you now have only question marks. After completing this level of analysis of your golf skills, you are ready to begin creating effective plans for every hole and every shot that you play.

The Psychology of Planning

To improve our understanding of the process of planning on the golf course, we conducted an on-course research study with our colleague Eddie O'Connor in September 1996. We wanted to study a golf hole that presented several interesting challenges, so we could observe how golfers developed strategies to handle those challenges. Our choice was the fourteenth hole of the Winnetka Golf Club, a very well-maintained public course located twenty miles north of Chicago in Winnetka, Illinois.

Our Research on Planning

Figure 4.1 shows what that hole looked like to golfers in September 1996. Due to construction on the regular tees that began just a few weeks before this study, golfers had to use the temporary tees shown in the illustration. Those temporary tees were located seventy-five yards in front of the regular tees. This rather dramatically changed the nature of the hole. Golfers who played the course regularly, many of whom have been playing it for many years, had to develop a new plan to manage this hole effectively.

Before reading our findings, take a few minutes to figure out how you would play this hole. Try answering the following four questions to guide your decision making. Please consider carefully not only how you would play the hole, but why you would follow that particular plan.

Planning to Play Hole #14 at the Winnetka Golf Club

- From which position did you want to approach the green?

Figure 4.1
The Fourteenth Hole at the Winnetka Golf Club

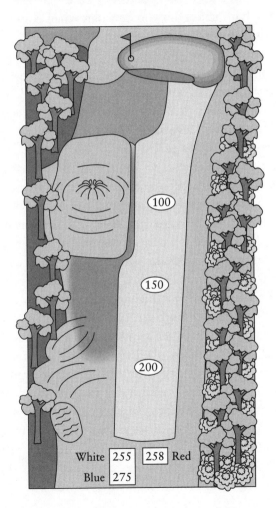

- Where did you want to hit your tee shot?
- What club would you use from the tee?
- What factors did you consider when constructing your plan?

Let's take a look at how your plan matched those of the 171 golfers we observed on a beautiful, sunny Sunday in early September. The temperature was in the low seventies and a variable breeze was blowing gently at three to ten miles per hour.

First and foremost, we wanted to know what clubs the golfers would choose for their tee shots. Recall how your own plan resulted in a specific club selection for the tee shot. We thought tallying club selections of the 171 golfers would tell us a lot about how golfers plan.

This hole, more than most, presents golfers with a wide array of options for their tee shots. Golfers could try to hit tee shots past the end of the pond on the left of the hole all the way up to the green. This would leave something between a half wedge and a chip for a second shot. Certainly playing for such a short second shot could prove very tempting. Another approach would be to use a relatively short iron off the tee in an attempt to place the ball between the 100- and 150-yard markers in the fairway. For most golfers this would leave a full wedge to mid-iron into the green.

We consulted with the very cooperative and skilled head golf professional at the Winnetka Golf Club, Steve

Patterson. We asked him to advise us of his opinion of the best plan for this hole for most golfers who play this course. Steve's opinion coincided exactly with our own.

We all concurred that the best approach for the vast majority of golfers would be to use a club from the tee that would place their balls between the 150-yard marker and approximately the 130-yard position in the fairway. This target takes the water on the left out of play. Golfers could not reach the water if they hit clubs that could only fly to the 130-yard point in the fairway. This approach also reduces the very serious risk of hitting the ball into the right tree hazard. Only low-handicappers who could be sure of carrying their tee shots safely past the end of the water hazard on the left could justify taking the risk of hitting a driver on this hole. For those who can safely carry their tee shots 240 yards or more with a fair amount of control (hence their low handicaps), it makes sense to go for it. Otherwise, hitting a driver—or any club that clearly brings both the water on the left and the tree hazard on the right very much into play—risks a severe penalty for very little reward. In contrast, laying up so that the second shot would be a wedge or a short- or mid-iron greatly weakens the strengths of the hole, and therefore makes it much easier to get to the green safely by the second (or third, depending on skill level) stroke.

We wondered what percentage of golfers would follow this plan—one that made sense to us and to the head professional at this course. We also wanted to see what would happen if we gave a second chance to golfers who hit drivers or other clubs that brought the hazards into play. We thought that golfers given this second chance who were advised to follow our more conservative plan would greatly improve their positions when compared to what happened with their original tee shots.

To score and analyze what happened to the tee shots, we had to create a method of assigning values to all possible positions on the hole. With the help of Steve Patterson, we assigned a range of values based on our collective best guesses as to what average golfers (those with handicaps between 16 and 20) would score if their tee shots landed in those positions. These positioning scores provided an objective means of evaluating the relative quality of each tee shot. For example, we thought that a ball hit in the fairway to a position 130 yards from the center of the green would yield an average score for an average golfer that is about 1.3 strokes better than a ball hit into the water hazard. That is why we valued the 130-yards-from-green in the fairway position at 5.3 versus the water ball at 6.6. Does that seem reasonable to you? To simplify the scoring further, we grouped these positions in the following way: excellent (expected score = 5 or less), average (expected score = 5 or 6), and very poor (expected score = 6 or more). Figure 4.2 shows the three groupings of positions.

Figure 4.2
Excellent, Average, and Very Poor Positions for Tee Shots
on the Fourteenth Hole at the Winnetka Golf Club

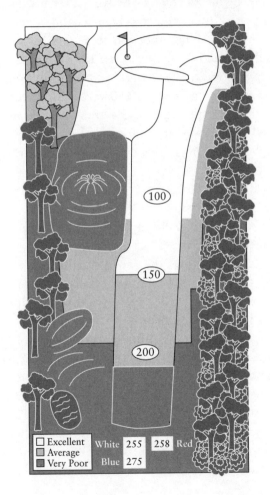

100

150

200

☐ Excellent   White 255   258 Red
☐ Average
■ Very Poor   Blue 275

In addition to recording initial club selections and ball positions off the tee, we recorded the position obtained by the 94 golfers who were given a second ball to hit. The golfers who received second chances and who used the White and Red tees were asked to hit shots that would go no more than 125 yards; the golfers who used the Blue tees were asked to hit shots that would travel no more than 150 yards. All golfers were given the specific target of the area near the brightly painted white 150-yard marker and just beyond it on the right side of the fairway, as shown in Figure 4.3.

Results

Guess what percentage of golfers elected to use their drivers on this hole? What do you think happened to their tee shots?

Figure 4.4 shows the range of clubs used by the golfers on that early September Sunday (shown in the figure as "Normal Golf"). Notice that a majority of golfers hit drivers. When the golfers followed our instructions (shown in the figure as "Smart Golf"), 82 percent of them hit 6-irons or less—versus 6 percent when playing Normal Golf. Out of the 171 golfers who played this hole on that day, four of them met the criteria of having handicaps of 5 or less and being capable of carrying the ball 240 yards. Taking these golfers into account, and using the clubs actually selected by the remainder of the golfers for ball 2, we created the Smart

Figure 4.3
Suggested Target Area for Tee Shots at the Fourteenth Hole
at the Winnetka Golf Club

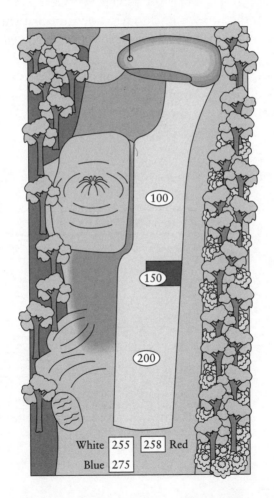

Golf data shown in Figure 4.4. *This analysis shows that 80 percent of the golfers selected the wrong club when playing Normal Golf!* You can see very clearly in Figure 4.4 that the two sets of club selections (the first without instructions, the second with instructions) showed only a 20 percent overlap!

We also wanted to see what happened to the tee shots during Normal Golf (80 percent dubious club selections) versus Smart Golf club selections. Figure

Figure 4.4
Club Selections—Normal Golf Compared to Smart Golf

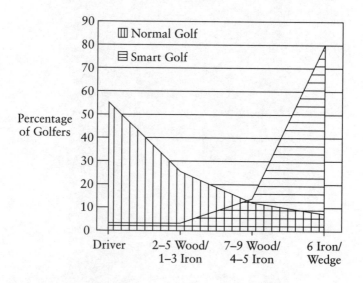

4.5 compares the tee shot positions when golfers used their initial club selections (Normal Golf) versus when they used the Smart Golf club selections for their second shots.

The figure dramatically illustrates the benefits of the planning strategy. Second ball positions were far better (and very significantly better in a statistical sense) than first ball positions. This observation held equally for golfers with low (less than 12), medium (13 to 24), and

Figure 4.5
Tee Shot Quality—Normal Golf Compared to Smart Golf

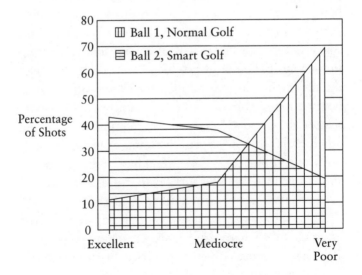

high (25 or over) handicaps. In fact, two-thirds of the golfers improved their positions using the Smart Golf instructions for their second balls. Even more impressive is the degree of improvement observed. "Excellent" positions went from 13 percent to 44 percent, "mediocre" positions from 18 percent to 37 percent, and "very poor" positions from 69 percent to 19 percent.

The low-handicappers (0 to 12) improved their scores by one-half stroke and the high-handicappers (25 and up) improved their scores by one-third stroke, on average. These may sound like small changes at first. Yet, half a stroke per hole averages out to nine strokes per round. This is a huge effect, especially for low-handicappers. Also, better ball positions were highly correlated with better scores, as you would expect. This suggests that the better ball positions associated with the second ball should produce better scores most of the time. This did not happen for every golfer, partly because many golfers used poor planning on their second or third shots. For example, many golfers hit too much club on their approach shots, resulting in poor positions. If Smart Golf planning had been used on all shots, not just the tee shots, even more dramatic improvements in scores would have occurred.

The results of this study very clearly support the impressions of many experienced teaching professionals. That is, most golfers would benefit from improving the planning aspects of their game.

Why Don't Golfers Plan Better?

Our research at the Winnetka Golf Club showed that 80 percent of golfers planned poorly. Yet, most golfers think of themselves as skilled strategists. This was especially obvious in the comments of many of the players during the course of the study we conducted at the fourteenth hole:

- *Super ball?* At least five golfers asked if the second balls provided to them were some new type of "super ball." In reality, we gave them reconditioned balls that cost approximately fifty cents each. At that price most golfers at Winnetka were hitting balls that cost four to six times as much as our so-called super balls.

- *Illogic in the face of logic: Part I.* A very cooperative and friendly 36-handicapper hit a 5-iron from the White tees. His ball took one bounce and landed in the pond on the left side of the fairway. After receiving his second ball with the Smart Golf instructions, he hit an 8-iron into the fairway approximately 155 yards from the middle of the green. After hitting this rather acceptable second shot, he asked about the purpose of the study. Dan told him, "Most people hit too much club here and you were a good example of that." He replied, "Not me." He seemed quite friendly about disagreeing with Dan's assertion. Nonetheless, he maintained his position that his 5-iron was the correct club to use—despite the results!

- *Illogic in the face of logic: Part II.* A fifteen-year-old junior golfer who reported a 28 handicap used a 3-wood off the tee. He put his ball about 80 yards from the green, but very near the right hazard (under some troublesome overhanging branches that could have affected his next shot). His second tee shot (using the Smart Golf instructions and a 7-iron) landed perfectly: 125 yards from the green in the middle of the fairway. When discussing the point of the study, he said, "So the point was to hit a more conservative shot?" We enthusiastically responded, "Exactly!" The junior golfer replied, "That is just why I hit a 3-wood instead of a driver—to be more conservative." We asked, "Yes, but did you notice the differences in the outcomes when you used the 7-iron versus the 3-wood? You illustrated very nicely the difference between a somewhat more conservative shot (3-wood) and a truly more conservative shot (7-iron) taking into account the strengths of the hole." He muttered, "Yeah, I guess I could see that a little." This young man viewed his second shot as only slightly better than his first one, if at all. Would you rather punch an 80-yard shot over a bunker through overhanging tree limbs from the rough or hit a 125-yard shot from a perfect lie in the fairway?

- *Seeking out unimportant information while ignoring critical facts.* At least twenty people asked exactly how far the tees were to the middle of the green.

The tees themselves were actually positioned five yards behind the clearly apparent yardage marker for both the White and Blue tees; two yards in front of the Red tee yardage sign. Still, quite a few people wanted to know exactly how far the hole was playing. Only one man asked or discussed with us the distance between the tees and the water that blanketed much of the left side of the fairway. We did not hear a single discussion among the golfers about the positioning of the water, and only one mentioned it to us. Yet most groups discussed the fact that the tees were five yards behind the yardage sign (or two yards in front for the Reds). In other words, the golfers were preoccupied with the distance to the middle of the green, instead of carefully analyzing the strengths of the hole. This again reflects an overly optimistic view that the hazards on the hole wouldn't (almost couldn't!) affect their shots.

• *The King Kong delusion.* Three groups of golfers, including no one with a handicap lower than 15, waited for the green to clear completely before hitting their tee shots. None of these players came anywhere near the green. In fact, none of them came within 100 yards of it. Interestingly, the narrowness, hardness, and elevation of the green were such that if a golfer somehow carried the ball 275 yards so it landed on the green, it would probably bounce into the hazard behind the green. This would result in an almost-guaranteed double bogey or worse.

• *Logic in the face of illogic: Part III.* While taking a lunch break, we overheard a conversation between two golfers that went something like this:

GOLFER 1: I hit 6-iron, wedge on #14 today. Guess what? After a perfect 6-iron, I hit my wedge about thirty feet! I swear that wedge didn't go further than that door over there.

GOLFER 2: You should hit a driver like I do on that hole.

GOLFER 1: I guess.

Just because a golfer mis-hits a particular shot, should that lead to a change in strategy? Notice that Golfer 2 seemed less concerned with the logic of how to plan to play a hole than with getting his friend to imitate him. Issues other than logic obviously can determine how golfers plan their golf shots.

Consider these questions based on this research:

• Why did golfers choose the wrong club 80 percent of the time?
• Why did so many golfers show concern about the exact yardage of the hole, while only one out of the whole group seemed concerned about the huge water hazard that practically covered the entire left side of the fairway?

- Why did at least five golfers think they played their second ball so much better than their first because the second one was some kind of "super ball"?
- Why did some golfers maintain that their initial club selections (which clearly produced worse outcomes) were still somehow better for them than the instructed club selection?

Fortunately, psychology research has provided answers to these seemingly mystifying questions. The following sections review some of the pertinent research and provide insights about why planning can go so far awry.

Cognitive Biases

During the past twenty-five years psychologists have conducted studies on common distortions in thinking and reasoning. These *cognitive biases* affect sport performance as they affect other areas of our lives. Cognitive biases such as overly positive views of ourselves and our skills are very typical of normal, healthy human thought. Research shows that depressed people tend to be sadder but wiser.

Golfers seem especially prone to these positive distortions in thinking. How many times have you and your friends looked at a very ominous darkening sky that a nongolfer (a normal person?) would see as an imminent sign of a major thunderstorm and said, "Do you see that blue sky over there on the horizon poking through? I think this is going to blow over." How many times have you heard golfers describe themselves at a handicap level that seemed completely inconsistent with their actual games—and far more skillful? If you could take a cold, hard—and dispassionately objective—look at how people play golf, you'd see evidence for rampant cognitive biases run amok!

Positive Illusions

Unfortunately, the illusions that serve our mental health so well can ruin our golf games. For this reason, it seems important to take a closer look at the nature of the positive illusions that most of us thrive on, and attempt to understand how they can influence our golf games. The upshot of this analysis is a system of planning that can reduce the unfortunate impact of positive illusions in golf—without destroying the useful aspects of those illusions.

Psychologists Shelly Taylor and Jonathan Brown categorized the positive illusions that affect most of us in three ways: unrealistic optimism, exaggerated perceptions of control or mastery, and overly positive self-evaluations. Unrealistic optimism occurs when people view the future with very thick rose-colored glasses. For example, college students report four times as many positive possibilities as negative possibilities for their futures. People also evaluate their chances of experiencing negative events such as having an automobile accident or becoming a crime victim as less likely for themselves than for their peers. People seem to be saying, "the future will be great, especially for me." Obviously, not everyone's future can be better than that of their peers. This shows that the optimism displayed by the average person is unrealistic or illusory.

A very interesting example of unrealistic optimism emerged in the largest and most comprehensive survey of middle age ever attempted. Researcher Paul Cleary recently reported that based on a nationally representative random sample of more than seven thousand men and women, people often underestimate risks to their physical health. Cleary noted that 70 percent of the smokers in the survey believed they had similar or lower risk of heart attack than others of their age. Even more remarkable, only 40 percent of the smokers believed that their risks of getting cancer were higher than average. Even among smokers who also had high blood pressure, a family history of heart attacks, and existing signs of heart disease (such as angina), less than half believed that their risks for heart attack were higher than average. People in this latter category (smokers with other very obvious risks for heart attack) are at least ten times more likely than average to experience a heart attack—yet they didn't see it that way (Azar, 1996).

In addition to unrealistic optimism, people seem to benefit from illusions of control. A host of studies on tasks and situations such as gambling show this effect. For example, people believe that if they personally throw dice, they can exert greater control of the outcome than if someone else throws the dice.

The final category of positive illusions described by Taylor and Brown is unrealistically positive views of the self. People tend to recall positive feedback and positive information about their personalities very efficiently and easily. Negative feedback is poorly understood and recalled. People also show poor recall for information regarding their failures in specific tasks compared to information about success in various tasks. How many times have your heard golfers talk about the great skill they exhibited when they hit their better shots? What happens when a shot goes awry? Golfers themselves—and television commentators—are notorious for blaming spike marks, sudden gusts of wind, mud on the ball, impossible lies, and even far more creative external events (would you believe sunspots?) for bad shots.

Jack Nicklaus, the best golfer in history, is a prime example of this style of thinking:

> In his prime during all his best years, Nicklaus never missed many putts that he needed to make. It's an absolute truth that nobody ever made as many putts that he *had* to make in dire situations, in large events, as Jack Nicklaus. I mean the guy sank crucial, killer putts for 20 years! I brought this up one

evening when we were having a chat. I was hoping to draw from him some deep dark secret about his putting. How could he explain it? Sheer luck? God's chosen golfer? What? He mulled it over for a moment, and finally looked at me in his matter-of-fact way, and said "I've never missed a putt in my *mind*" [Jenkins, 1994, pp. xix-xx].

Nicklaus expected to make every putt, which he certainly did not do. He also attributed almost every critical misputt to spike marks or some external condition. At least that is our impression. We can't recall a single incident when Nicklaus missed a critical putt that he attributed to his own lack of skill or lack of practice or basic inadequacy as a golfer. He was always very quick to find an external factor to which he could attribute his problematic outcomes.

Why do positive illusions persist? Taylor and Brown's analysis provides an answer to this puzzling question. They quoted Pulitzer prizewinner Samuel Beckett, "Because the world is an uncertain and frightening place to live in, people create positive life-affirming illusions to enable them to cope with their existential terror." Their own answer is also worth reviewing carefully:

The individual who responds to negative, ambiguous, or unsupportive feedback with a positive sense of self, a belief in personal efficacy, and an optimistic sense of the future will be happier, more caring, and more productive than the individual who perceives the same information accurately and integrates it into his or her view of the self, the world, and the future. In this sense, the capacity to develop and maintain positive illusions may be thought of as a valuable human resource to be nurtured and promoted, rather than an error-prone processing system to be corrected. In any case, these illusions help make each individual's world a warmer and more attractive and beneficent place in which to live [1988, p. 205].

Taylor and Brown make a good case for the many benefits of positive illusions. Positive illusions can improve overall adjustment and functioning, but they can also cause problems on the golf course. In other words, what's good for your mental health is not good for your handicap.

Five Common Distortions in Thinking That Affect Golfers

Take a look at Table 4.1. It includes important information about five common problems that affect judgments people make in everyday life. These distortions in thinking clearly affect the quality of the plans golfers use. These categories of distortions certainly overlap with the three aspects of positive illusions identified earlier (unrealistic optimism, illusions of control, and overly positive self-evaluations). Yet the five distortions in Table 4.1 also include other types of difficulties in making judgments beyond these three categories. The names and descriptions of these categories of distortions may also help you see some problematic nuances in your own planning strategies.

Some of the categories of distortions in thinking play a more central role in creating problems for golfers than others. Take another look at Table 4.1 and identify the categories that you believe create the greatest number of difficulties for you and your regular playing partners. Confusing correlation with causation and using information as a result of availability or sampling bias are certainly among the most dangerous distortions in thinking for golfers. In addition to the examples in the table, let's consider a few other examples of these distortions in thinking and their impact on golf scores.

Problems with judgments that pertain to correlation as opposed to causation loom very large when people analyze components of their own golf swings or those of their friends. Skilled professional golf teachers have learned to identify the primary causes of mis-hit shots. These professionals can separate the primary causes from the *correlates,* that is, the factors that simply happen at the same time.

The best single example of this is the oft-heard statement, "Oops, you really moved your head on that one. You gotta really keep that head down." This is one

Table 4.1
Five Common Categories of Distorted Thinking That Affect Golfers

Name of Distortion	Description	Example
Anchoring	Failure to take into account new information when forming an opinion	You hit the driver well on a particular hole the first three times you played the hole; the next ten times you played the hole the driver tee shots landed in hazards five times. You continue to use the driver because you ignore the more recent problems.
Availability	Using information that is easily accessible from memory rather than information that is appropriate to the situation	Remembering the great shot where you used a fairway wood to escape a shallow bunker, while ignoring the outcomes when using that club from fairway bunkers with high lips.
Correlation Confused with Causation	Mistakenly believing that factor A caused factor B just because factor A and B occurred at the same time	Deciding that practice interferes with your golf performance because you played better at the start of the season when you didn't practice at all than during the middle of the season when you practiced regularly.
Gambler's Fallacy	Believing that an event is more likely because it has not occurred for a while	Deciding that you are due for a streak of very good putting because your putting has been lousy for a long time.
Sampling Bias	Failing to consider characteristics of the larger sample from which a particular observation was drawn	Deciding that you hit your average 7-iron shot 150 yards even though you really hit only your best 7-iron shots (the top 10 percent) that distance.

Source: Summaries of the research that identified these distortions in thinking and analyzed their impact on behaviors and attitudes include Eysenck (1993), Kahneman, Slovic, and Tversky (1982), Nisbett (1993), Nisbett and Ross (1980), and Weist, Finney, and Ollendick (1992).

of the most widely used examples of misinformation on golf courses throughout the world. Excessive head movement during a golf swing is often a result of another problem in the golf swing, not a cause of the mishit. It is normal for the head to move on the backswing or as a result of your turn or pivot. When golfers force their heads to stay immobile, they often cause a *reverse weight shift*. The reverse weight shift occurs when the golfer leans toward the target side of the ball when extending his or her arms away from the ball during the backswing. Then, as the club approaches the ball, centrifugal force causes the upper body (including the head) to move, sometimes dramatically, away from the target. This usually results in a very weak hit. The head movement doesn't cause the mis-hit in this case. Trying to keep the head still can cause both the mis-hit and the head movement.

Many of the advertisements in golf magazines rely on the types of distorted thinking that Table 4.1 describes. How many times have you read ads saying that if you hit this club—or use this ball or wear these shoes—you will improve your scores or your distance? If you kept switching clubs and balls every time you saw an ad that "guarantees" another 10 percent improvement, in a few years you could easily outhit Tiger Woods. For example, if you hit your average drive 200 yards ten years ago, adding 10 percent each year would yield these results: year two = 220, year three = 242, year four = 266, year five = 293, year six = 322, year seven = 354, year eight = 389, year nine = 428, and year ten = 471! Just think, all you have to do is switch from forged blades to musclebacks to perimeter weighted irons to graphite shafts to 400+ dimpled golf balls and so on—and you'll hit tee shots on average further than anyone who's ever touched a golf ball! Even the more modest promise of ten yards per equipment change could have you hitting them nose to nose with Tiger or Laura before long.

Technology has certainly improved golf equipment. Golfers now have a greater variety from which to choose as well as far more customized possibilities. Is improvement automatic with the newer, improved models? For some, yes.

But advertisements often promise more than they can deliver when selling golf equipment, cars, and all other products. The distortion in thinking known as "correlation, not causation" helps advertisers succeed where logic fails. We see that Tiger Woods or Laura Davies uses a certain club or a certain ball. They play extremely well. Therefore, so this thinking goes, if we use that club or that ball, we too can play somewhat closer to the level of these outstanding golfers. This thinking ignores the fact that these professional athletes have spent their entire lives hitting golf balls, practicing hitting golf balls, getting instruction on how to hit golf balls, reading about how to hit golf balls, and playing golf. While these players were hitting thousands upon thousands of balls and focusing almost exclusively on their golf games, you were working in some other domain, raising a family, going to school, living your life. The specific ball or club that the best golfers use is not what causes them to play at an outstanding level.

Nondepressed golfers tend to remember their more glorious moments on the golf course, while having rather fuzzy memories of the shots that they barely got off the ground. This use of the availability and sampling bias distortions in thinking (see Table 4.1) leads many golfers to think such things as "I hit my driver better than I hit my 3-wood." These golfers may simply remember their better driver shots better than their better 3-woods (availability bias). Or, they may not have hit enough 3-woods to compare fairly to the number of drivers they hit (sampling bias). The laws of physics suggest that statements favoring drivers over 3-woods are probably inaccurate for most golfers. The straighter face on the driver and its longer shaft make it more difficult to hit than the 3-wood for most golfers. While there certainly are some exceptions to this principle, generally golfers hit more lofted and shorter clubs better than less lofted and longer clubs.

Whenever your thinking leans toward defying the laws of physics, please consider testing it out more thoroughly. That is, instead of simply accepting your own view of how much better you hit your driver than your 3-wood, go out and hit ten, twenty, or thirty balls with each club. Carefully calculate how far each shot went both in terms of distance and accuracy. Then—based on data, not flawed impressions—decide which club you hit better. Also, take your test to the golf course. Which clubs do you keep in play more than 50 percent of the time?

Our cognitive biases keep us from understanding how our clubs usually perform and this distorted thinking usually extends to our analysis of our overall game. Even the great Bobby Jones succumbed to these distortions:

> Golf is also a game of temperament and, for some of us, even of temper. The whole thing seems so simple, and our better performances seem so easy. Invariably we become convinced that our best shots are merely normal and that our lowest rounds represent that thing we call our "game." Any regression from this standard is therefore intolerable.
>
> I remember that I was a very young man when I first played East Lake, my home course, in 63. Afterward, I confided to my father that I had mastered the secret of the game and that I should never go above 70 again. [The] next day I had to work my head off to get around in 77 [Jones, 1954, p. xiv].

🏌 Four Principles of Effective Planning in Golf

When you consider the results of the Winnetka study and our analysis of why golfers suffer from positive illusions, what are your conclusions? Do you see yourself as a victim of positive illusions on the golf course, at least some of the time?

If you do see the impact of positive illusions in your game, you could use an alternative planning strategy to counter those illusions. Our research, teaching, and other experiences have shown us four principles of effective planning in golf: personal par, conservation, wide first, and safety first. If you use these principles consistently, you will find your scores decreasing. These principles essentially allow you to fight your own tendency toward positive illusions on the golf course. If you don't use them or strategies very much like them, we believe the natural tendency toward positive illusions will take over—resulting in poor judgments and higher scores. The following provides an infamous example of this point, as it affected one of the best players in the world in 1996.

Greg Norman's Infamous Collapse at the 1996 Masters: Another Victim of Positive Illusions?

Greg Norman began a perfect Sunday morning with a six-shot lead over Nick Faldo at the 1996 Masters. Norman's

78 in perfect weather was certainly one of the highest
rounds ever posted by the leader of a major championship
on the final day of the tournament. Why did it happen?

In our opinion, Norman's natural aggressiveness was
not well suited to the moment. Yet in some of this post-Mas-
ters interviews he suggested that he hit only two bad shots.
How could the best golfer in the world shoot 78 in perfect
conditions by missing only two shots? He hit tee shots into
water hazards on both par 3s on the back nine, badly
pulled several approach shots, thinned at least one chip,
and stroked several poor putts.

Norman's 78 included far more than two poor shots—
unless one uses a positive illusion to do the math. Most
experts also viewed his swing as technically sound, even
during that disastrous performance. He did not use a plan
focused on the centers of the fairways and the safer spots
on the greens. He used a positive illusion that encouraged
him to think he should go for great shots when he didn't
need great shots.

Norman is a great player, certainly among the best
players in the world in the 1990s. But even great players struggle with course management sometimes. Norman could improve his play under extreme pressure by
giving more consideration to the Smart Golf planning
principles. Let's take a more detailed look at those principles—beginning with the most critical one for most
golfers, personal par, followed by three that could benefit Greg Norman as well as beginning golfers: conservation, wide first, and safety first. You may find in your

own game that you adhere to one, two, or three of the four principles. Working on the others could be the key to lowering your scores, particularly when playing under pressure.

Personal Par

Try to create a personal par for each hole to begin your planning for that hole. By using a personal par, you can plan the hole most effectively, developing a plan to match your current ability. If the hole has many strengths (is potentially quite punitive) you certainly have to take the handicap listings on the scorecard very seriously. This means if you get a stroke or two on a particular hole that has many strengths, the scorecard may read 4, but your personal par would be 5 or 6. With this analysis as a base of thinking, determine which club to use for your tee shots and approach shots that should avoid the trouble on the hole—even if this requires hitting a shot of relatively modest length off the tee. This approach will get you to the green in regulation for your personal par more often than simply using the par on the scorecard as a guidepost for your plan.

Conservation

The conservation principle addresses the risk-to-reward aspect of planning. If you wish to have your rewards outweigh your risks, you will generally use a conservative approach. In other words, when facing a choice between a more conservative play and a less conservative play, you will lower your scores in the long run by using the more conservative approach most of the time.

Conservation argues against the "go for it" approach used by Tin Cup in the 1996 movie of the same name. Conservation suggests taking a look at your lie, your situation, and the strengths and weaknesses of the hole versus your own strengths and weaknesses, and taking as little risk as possible. This attitude helps counter our natural tendencies toward positive illusions. We tend to remember our better shots and outcomes and think of our abilities as more advanced than they really are. Whenever you face a choice between more and less conservative plays, try to remember the principle of conservation.

Another aspect of the conservation principle concerns hitting shots that you have actually practiced. Just because you have seen another player try something and make it work or you have read about something recently, that doesn't mean you can make it work on the golf course today. If you haven't tried and practiced a flop shot recently, you would be better off chipping the ball than attempting your first flop shot during a critical moment in a round of golf.

You can be sure that Ben Hogan followed this principle of conservation; he practically invented it:

Ben has one technique in his club selection which brands him as a conservative. On an approach shot, he tries to make certain he is short of the green rather than over it. At Carnoustie in Scotland [where Hogan won the 1953 British Open], all the trouble lies behind the green as it does in 90 percent of the courses here in America. . . . who's to say this conservative approach is the wrong one? Not I certainly. Course charting is automatic for the careful fellow who selects the proper club. When Hogan goes into the bag for a certain stick it is a safe bet he has looked over the area he is shooting for with a telescopic eye. He plans his shot carefully before swinging. A number of times he has been criticized for taking too much time with shots. They call him the surveyor, and Ben resents it. "That's a brutal word to tag on a golfer," he says. "When I look a course over, I try to figure it out. I want to know what's going to happen when my shot hits the ground. I want to check the grass as well as the distance to the green or my particular objective. Now what's wrong with that?"

If necessary, he'll pace off the distance from where his ball lies to the spot where he thinks it will come down. While he is doing that, he'll investigate the grass and every shrub, tree, bunker and depression along the way. In the 1953 open, he strolled 250 yards uphill on the 17th, to get an idea of what would happen when his ball hit the ground. If he's trying to whack that ball over trees to save ground on a dog-leg hole or he feels that he can drive over a bunker, he will always make sure just what is behind these obstacles. He knows what's going to happen on the other end of the shot [Demaret, 1954, p. 259].

Wide First

Narrow strips of fairway and tight pin placements are strengths of golf holes. Large, flat areas of the green and wide areas in the fairways are weaknesses of those holes. If you aim for the wide parts of the fairways and greens, you give yourself more room for error.

Some players find it useful to adopt a rule about when to go for a relatively tightly tucked pin. For example, professionals may aim for a pin with only fifteen or twenty feet around it from as far away as 200 yards. High-handicappers probably would do better simply to aim for the widest part of the green under every circumstance, except when they are in chipping range. Medium-handicappers may have a certain yardage that would allow them to go for a relatively tight pin fairly safely. Perhaps when medium-handicappers are within 8-iron and less range, such shots become reasonable. Those with lower handicaps may be able to extend this to 6-irons or 5-irons depending on their skill and comfort levels with those clubs.

The notion of "wide first" implies that you pick a specific target before hitting every shot. This is crucial. You can attempt to envision your own green in the middle of a fairway and hit for that green. You can pick a smaller spot if one is easily identifiable from the tee. You may find a shading difference in the grass or certain other markings in the fairway that can help you aim more specifically. In a similar vein, it helps to find a certain area of the green that you can see to use as a specific target.

Safety First

A famous golf saying applies here: *When playing safe, play safe.* In other words, the principle of safety first argues that when you get in some trouble on the golf course, go for the more conservative, safer means of escape whenever possible. This approach yields lower scores when compared to attempting to squeeze every extra yard out of a difficult position.

Do you remember the last time you attempted to escape from trouble and put your escape shot into a bunker, water hazard, or back into the trees? These moments can create very unpleasant memories that are unfortunately rather short-lived for most of us. If you can find a way of accepting and using the safety-first principle, you will learn to accept a penalty situation for what it is, rather than multiplying the penalty.

Plans to Play Dubsdread

In this section, you will see illustrations showing four holes from Dubsdread, one of the premier golf courses in the world. PGA players contest the Motorola Western

Open on this course, located thirty miles southwest of Chicago in Lemont, Illinois. *Golf Digest* consistently ranks this course in the top twenty-five in the country and considers it one of the hundred most difficult courses to play.

We have constructed four composite golfers to help us show you methods of developing effective plans to play Dubsdread. These four composites are based on our students, friends, and associates. Here is a brief description of each of them, followed by Table 4.2, which lists their standard yardages by club.

- *Tim—low handicap.* Tim is forty-three years old. He owns a small, successful business and plays at least fifty rounds of golf per year. Tim hits the ball a long way, but struggles sometimes on and around the green. Tim practices infrequently, but plays so much that he keeps his game reasonably sharp during the golf season (about six months long in Chicago).

- *Jay—medium handicap.* Jay is a twenty-four-year-old newly graduated professional. He is single, affording him perhaps more opportunities to play and practice than some of his more senior friends. He takes advantage of this by hitting a couple of buckets at least several times a week and practicing his short game as well. Jay is capable of hitting relatively long tee shots (in the

250- to 270-yard range), but he also tends to spray them around. His irons are the strength of his game and his putting goes hot and cold.

- *Leslie—medium handicap*. Leslie is a tall woman (five feet ten inches) who has considerable athletic talent. She was a distance runner and avid tennis player in high school. She also enjoyed a very competitive amateur volleyball career. Leslie is forty-nine years old, works as an attorney in Philadelphia, and has children in high school and college. She makes time for rounds of golf at least once per week during the golf season (seven months long) and practices by going to a driving range at least twice per week. She also does some putting around her office as a means of relaxing and taking a break from the stress of her job.

- *Al—high handicap*. Al is sixty-eight years old and a recent retiree. He lives in Florida and plays golf all year round. He played to as low as a 16 in his younger days, but his loss of hand strength and flexibility have resulted in a higher handicap in more recent years. Al enjoys playing more than practicing, but he does spend some time at least every other day hitting balls and working on his short game.

Let's take a look at some reasonable personal pars and plans for each of these four players for all four

Table 4.2
Comparison of Composite Golfers

	Tim	Jay	Leslie	Al
Age:	43	24	49	68
Handicap:	6	13	15	25
Tees used:	Blue	White	White	Red
Club yardages				
D	280	250	225	210
3W	NA	220	205	190
4W	240	NA	NA	NA
5W	NA	200	290	180
7W	NA	190	180	170
9W	NA	NA	NA	160
2	220	NA	NA	NA
3	210	190	170	NA
4	200	180	160	NA
5	185	170	150	155
6	170	160	140	145
7	160	150	130	135
8	150	140	120	125
9	140	130	110	115
PW	125	115	100	100
SW	105	100	80	80
LW	75	70	60	60

Note: NA = not applicable.

holes on Dubsdread. Before reading the plans for our hypothetical golfers, why not look at the diagram of each hole—Figures 4.6 through 4.9—carefully and construct your own plan. Then see how your plan matches up with the plans of our four golfers. Imagine that the flag is located in the center of each green.

Hole #1

Dubs establishes its character in the challenges of this very first hole, accentuated by the decision required for the very first shot. It's a classic strategic hole in that it offers a major reward to those skilled enough (brave enough? foolish enough?) to attempt to cut off the corner of the dogleg with their tee shots. Successfully cutting that corner can yield a much shorter approach into a large, two-tiered, heavily bunkered green. Trying to cut the corner and failing to do so would leave little doubt in your mind about the appropriateness of the course's name, Dubsdread (accent on the dread).

Your Plan

Smart Golf

Figure 4.6
Hole #1 at Dubsdread

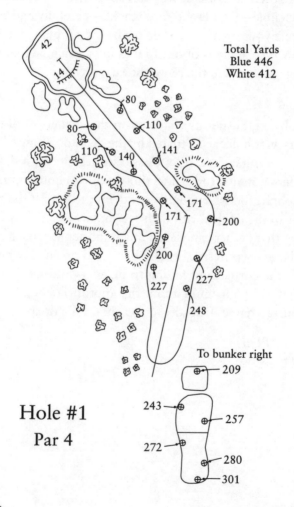

Total Yards
Blue 446
White 412

To bunker right

Hole #1
Par 4

Tim's Plan

Tim knew he played a draw shot that would go well with the left dogleg of this hole. His thoughts went to the approach shot first. He realized that he wanted no more than a 7-iron if at all possible coming into this challenging green. He also realized that since the hole carried a 9-handicap and he played to a 6, he got no strokes on this hole. However, he knew that the fairways were actually larger than they appear on the diagram. What Tim wanted was a shot off the tee that would put him within 160 yards or less. He realized that his normal tee shot—heading toward the widest part of the fairway (front of the right bunker)—would have an excellent chance of landing in that right bunker. This would produce a probable bogey, if not worse. On the other hand, his handicap, skill level, and usual flight of the ball suggested that he could aim for the left side of the fairway and attempt to draw the ball in from the right bunker. He could even aim toward the small part of the fairway beyond the 171-yard markers. This would leave him with the desired approach shot, between 160 and 140 yards.

If his drive did not follow the desired pathway, he could always scramble out of one of the bunkers into short iron approach range and play for the bogey—not too bad on a hole like this. This plan might seem to defy the principles of conservation and wide first (as it aims for a relatively distant and narrow part of the fairway). Yet Tim's personal par gave him no extra stroke on this hole. Given that and the nature of his ball flight and the strengths of his game (for example, his driving), he decided this hole seemed well set up for him to go for the par.

Jay's Plan

Jay did get a stroke on this hole. His starting point was the 243-yard marker, which brought the right bunker into play for his typical drive (240 to 260 yards). He had to decide whether to make this a three-shot par 4 (turning it into a personal par 5) or to try to hit a solid drive and a long second shot into the large green to go for the par. Jay knew he played a fade that would not set up well for this hole. Jay also recognized his strength as a good bunker player, not particularly intimidated by the bunkers around the green, so he could go for a long second shot without worrying too much about hitting a decent bunker shot. This thinking led him to decide to play his 3-wood off the tee, taking the right bunker out of play. He realized that this might leave him with a shot of 200 yards into a very large green. He knew he could usually count on being a good fairway wood player, which made him willing to gamble on hitting the green instead of the bunkers on his second shot. Thus he decided not to make this a personal par 5 but to make it a personal par 4½.

Jay's plan appropriately considers his strengths (fairway woods and bunker play). Although he got a stroke on this hole, he thought he might not need it as the hole's strengths did not include out-of-bounds or water hazards, which carry much more severe penalties than bunkers. Thus he decided to turn it into a par 4½ and see if he could negotiate a long second shot into the large green. This is again a sensible plan taking into account the relative strengths and weaknesses of Jay's game versus the hole's strengths and weaknesses.

Leslie's Plan

Leslie knew her relatively long drives—regularly in the 220-yard range—would make the 209 yards from her Red tee starting point to the bunker on the right a major factor in her plan. Unlike Jay, she wanted to stay out of the bunker, so she converted the hole into a personal par 5. Since she gets a handicap stroke on this hole, a personal par of 5 was a good choice. She decided to use a 5-wood off the tee, completely taking the right bunker out of play while aiming for the right side of the fairway (wide first). She then planned to hit enough club to put her between 80 and 110 yards out—perhaps using a wedge for the second shot, as she was confident about her wedges and short irons. This plan set up a fairly easy third shot into a large green.

Al's Plan

Al decided on a plan similar to Leslie's. He would start at the 243-yard marker, and use the one stroke he gets on this hole for a definite personal par 5. He planned to use a 5-wood off the tee, his most comfortable club, aiming for the wide part of the fairway. This should leave him with 250 yards to go to the middle of the green. He could comfortably hit his 9-wood approach leaving him with approximately 90 yards into the green. Given the extra tension of the first hole, it was a good idea not to take chances. This relatively conservative plan should leave Al feeling reasonably confident and ready to play the rest of the round.

Hole #12

This is a 200-yard par 3, intimidating even for the best players in the world. When Steve Stricker was running away with the tournament in 1996, he said immediately after the round that the tee shot on this hole was the only thing he feared on the back nine on Sunday. Although you cannot see it on the diagram, the green sits atop a ten-foot elevation. Around the green is nothing but trouble. The slopes are quite severe and any ball missing the green has an excellent chance of landing in a tree hazard.

Your Plan

Figure 4.7
Hole #12 at Dubsdread

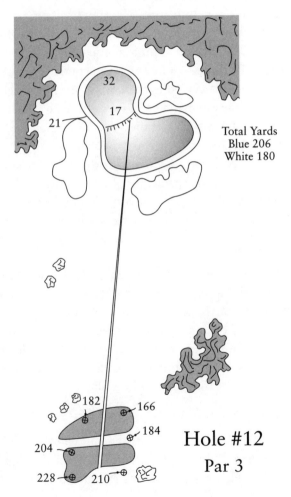

Total Yards
Blue 206
White 180

Hole #12
Par 3

Tim's Plan

Tim realized that he had to hit the ball 180 yards to get past the front bunkers, but the elevation of the tee meant that it wouldn't require a normal shot for that length. Tim wanted to hit a shot just far enough to clear the bunker, so he wanted as much control of the club as possible. He decided to choose a 7-iron in order to hit the ball approximately 175 yards (downhill) with good control. He aimed for the very middle of the widest portion of the green toward the front.

This plan certainly takes into account the wide-first principle and the principle of conservation. Tim realized that he could score a very big number if he hit the ball over the green or into the tree hazard on this hole.

Jay's Plan

Jay did not get a stroke on this hole. He wanted to go for the 3. He realized that he needed to hit a shot that would normally go approximately 160 yards on a flat terrain to clear the front bunker, aiming toward the right front center of the green (wide first). He chose a 6-iron, which he intended to hit smoothly, aiming it directly over the front right bunker.

Leslie's Plan

Leslie also did not get a stroke and wanted to play for the 3. She decided to hit a 5-iron to clear the right front bunker. She, too, chose less rather than more club to avoid the probable disaster that would occur if the shot went long.

Al's Plan

Al played this hole for a personal par 4. That took a lot of the intimidation out of the tee shot. He elected to use a 9-iron off the tee to leave himself a full pitching wedge into the right portion of the front of the green (wide first). Al simply didn't have enough confidence in his bunker game to attempt to go for this green in one shot.

Hole #15

This hole presents some real challenges, perhaps more than what first appears in the diagram. For example, the hole plays longer than the yardage listed because it plays uphill most of the way. Also, the tee shot can intimidate many golfers because it is over a deep ravine for the first 180 yards (from the Blue tees).

Your Plan

Figure 4.8
Hole #15 at Dubsdread

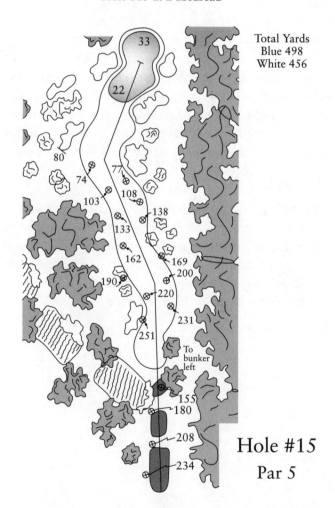

Total Yards
Blue 498
White 456

Hole #15
Par 5

Tim's Plan

Tim decided to hit a 4-wood off the tee because he knew he was playing this as a three-shot personal par 5. Also, the additional loft of the 4-wood took his concerns away from the ravine that seemed to stare at him from the tee. He knew that the 4-wood might bring the left bunker in the fairway into play, given that he can hit his 4-wood 240 yards. However, he figured that hitting uphill made it very unlikely that he would actually get the full 240-yard distance from his 4-wood. He hoped to hit a second shot 162 to 170 yards (6- or 7-iron) so as to get to the relatively wide part of the fairway flanked by the 103- and 108-yard markers. He planned to aim to the left side of the fairway to give himself a better approach to the green and to keep himself away from the woods and bunkers on the right.

Jay's Plan

Jay figured this hole probably got its very low handicap because of the ravine in front and the tree line and out-of-bounds areas on the right. If he could get the ball on the fairway off the tee, the functional handicap would go way up. Jay's skill level made this probable. He decided to consider the hole a personal par 5— especially if the tee shot landed safely.

Jay chose a 5-wood tee shot to stay short of the bunker on the left (208 yards from the White tees) and to have enough loft to clear the ravine easily. He planned to use the wide-first principle by aiming for the 103-yard marker with his lay-up second shot (a 6- or 7-iron), and for the middle of the green with his third.

Leslie's Plan

Due to the low handicap of the hole from the Red tees (2), Leslie realized that she might need to use another stroke somewhere along the line on this hole. Yet, like Jay, she knew that if her 4-iron tee shot was safe, she could translate this from a personal par 6 to a 5.

Leslie's chief focus was to hit a club that she could confidently get over the ravine and into decent playing position. The hole was playing approximately 430 yards from the Red tees. When Leslie teed it up from the marker indicated by the number 180, she elected to hit a 4-iron (her 160-yard club) to make sure her ball would stay out of the left bunker. She expected to have to hit between a 4-iron and a 7-wood for her second shot to get to the 100-yard marker in the fairway.

Al's Plan

Al understood that he got two strokes on this hole. However, he felt confident that the could clear the ravine in front of the tee box with his trusty 7-wood. Depending on his lie and position after the tee shot, he could then attempt to hit another 150- to 175-yard shot or go for a more conservative series of 9-iron and wedge shots. This more conservative route would get him to the green in four, giving him an opportunity to make his personal par 6. Both of these plans seemed reasonable, albeit less than maximally conservative.

Al's plan was conservative enough to yield a fairly good chance of making a 6 or at worst a 7. Al did appreciate the difficulties of the first shot as indicated by the hole's handicap. This helped him keep his expectations for score on this hole to a modest level. For example, Al realized that many high-handicappers do put their tee shots into the ravine in front of the tee box. He thought to himself, "If that occurs, I will just drop a ball behind the hazard and use a middle or short iron to get it across the hazard; I won't try to get fancy." This is a good example of a safety-first plan.

Hole #18

This hole more than deserves its 8 handicap listing. Its many strengths include its length (448 yards from the Blues), the out-of-bounds on the right, a rather tight fairway—which also slants sharply toward the water for the last 130 yards—and a relatively small green surrounded by a hillside (miss left and you're in the water). The out-of-bounds markers on the right side are actually closer than they appear on the diagram, as well. In addition, very tall trees block part of the fairway on the right side, and there are fairway bunkers both left and right and very much in range for some tee-shots. Once you get to the green, you find it slopes severely from back to front.

Figure 4.9
Hole #18 at Dubsdread

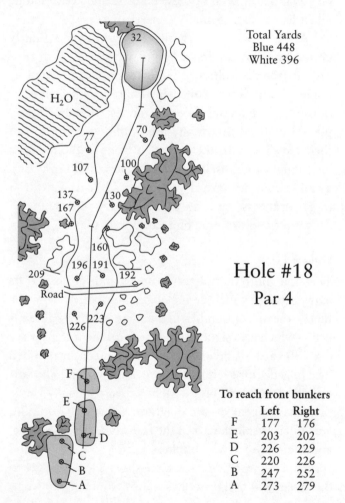

Total Yards
Blue 448
White 396

H₂O

32

77

70

107

100

137

130

167

160

196 191

192

209

Road

226 223

F

E

D

C

B

A

Hole #18
Par 4

To reach front bunkers

	Left	Right
F	177	176
E	203	202
D	226	229
C	220	226
B	247	252
A	273	279

Your Plan

Tim's Plan

Tim realized that if he hit one of his longer tee shots, it would have to land in a very small target area if he was to have a reasonable shot at this difficult green. That is, it would have to land on the left side of the fairway, between the bunkers on both the left and right sides of the fairway. If his ball landed slightly to the right of the center line of that fairway, he would quite possibly have to hit over the large overhanging trees on the right side. If his ball landed slightly to the left it would probably go into the bunker guarding the left side of the fairway.

He settled on a plan that used the principles of conservation and wide first. Even though the handicap on the scorecard says 8 and Tim plays to a 6, Tim wisely understood that his personal par was 5. He decided to hit a 5-iron tee shot. If this shot went 180 yards, it would land in the wide part of the fairway in front of the road. He knew that he could follow this up with a short iron second shot that could easily clear the trees on the right side. This short iron (perhaps a 9-iron) would land him in wedge range. He figured he could still scramble for the par if he could get his final approach close to the pin.

This plan makes effective use of the conservation principle. Tim realized that if he hooked or pulled his tee shot, he could easily put his next shot into the water that runs all along the left side of the fairway. A mishit to the right could also lead to a very large number, not the way he wanted to finish.

Jay's Plan

Jay, like Tim, realized that the strengths of this hole could easily overcome his game. He also did not want to end the round by having the golf course prove itself the master. Thus Jay realized that a personal par 5 would be a very good score on this hole.

Jay also elected to hit a 5-iron tee shot. He felt more confident in his 5-iron than in his 4- or 3-iron. He also realized that he didn't need the extra distance on this hole. If he hit his 5-iron reasonably well, he would land his ball somewhere near the 226-yard marker on the left side of the fairway. He could then hit a 9-iron second shot, leaving himself a pitching wedge or a sand wedge into the middle of the green.

Leslie's Plan

At 365 yards from the Red tees, this hole presented Leslie with the same challenges and same personal par 5 that it presented to Tim and Jay. It just wasn't worth it to her to attempt to hit a driver past the 160- and 167-yard markers. She also elected to hit a 5-iron, leaving her with a little more than 200 yards into the green. She too planned to hit a short iron second shot so that she could have a pitching wedge or sand wedge approach shot.

Al's Plan

He realized that this was one hole for which a bogey represented a very good score for him (personal birdie). He got two strokes on this hole. Yet he believed that he had a good chance of getting his personal birdie. Al decided to hit a 7-wood off the tee. If he hit this straight and solidly, he would have approximately 230 yards or so into the green. He could follow that with a 7-iron and pitching wedge or 9-iron, landing him on the green in three shots. He thought the 7-wood had a better chance of going straight than the 5-wood, even though he would have preferred the 5-wood's distance on this hole. An extra ten yards or so from the less lofted club did not seem worth it to him—it would violate the principle of conservation.

Further Reflections on Effective Plans

How did your plans contrast with those of Tim, Jay, Leslie, and Al? You probably saw the plans of our four composite golfers as quite conservative. After all, if you recall the results of the Winnetka study, most golfers do not play with conservative club selections off the tees. In fact, if you think about it, how many times have you seen anyone hit a short iron or even a middle iron off the tee at a challenging par 4? Yet, the plans of all our composite golfers (including a long-hitting low-handicapper) included holes where they used exactly that strategy. When accuracy of the tee shot has great importance (and deviations from a straight shot can lead to severe penalties), this approach simply plays the odds the best.

You can also see that the plans that we constructed tend to move backward from the green. That is, we took a look at the greens and decided which approach shot was warranted based on the nature of that green. If the green was particularly small or severely protected in a very strong manner, higher handicappers especially need to find some way of coming into that green with a short iron in their hands. On the other hand, when the green is a bit friendlier (more open), longer approach shots can work. Additional considerations that many golfers fail to include in their plans are the narrowness and the degree of protection in various portions of the fairway. On the eighteenth hole, for example, the best landing area for the tee shot was especially narrow and tightly guarded by both trees and bunkers. Also, on that hole, the risk of miscuing on the approach shot is very severe because of the water to the left of the fairway and the out-of-bounds and trees to the right. These considerations led to particularly conservative strategies on that hole.

If you find these recommendations too conservative, why not try them out a few times to give them a chance? Put these ideas to a systematic test and then you will see their benefits (or weaknesses) most clearly.

Reasonable Risks

Thus far Smart Golf planning has emphasized almost a right-wing conservative approach; we stressed personal par, conservation, and the other principles to help you avoid the natural tendency to risk too much too often. Yet part of golf's great appeal comes from the opportunities it presents for selective gambling. These opportunities help keep the game fun and exciting.

You can take reasonable risks and still play Smart Golf. Consider the following tempting scenario and decide how you would handle it:

You have a medium handicap, like our composite golfers Jay or Leslie. You are playing the par 5 fifteenth hole at Dubsdread for the first time. It's the number 4 (or 2 from the Red tees) handicap hole with an intimidating 180-yard gorge staring at you on the tee.

Imagine that you've been playing just great, in the zone. The game feels easy. Your tee shots, particularly those hit with your driver, have been sailing long and straight. The tee boxes are set up on the short side on this day. You think, "If I hit a really good tee shot with my driver, I could get close in two shots." On the other hand, your personal par for the hole is 6. You only need to get to the green in four shots to "par" it. Do you really want to gamble at this point in such a great round and put aside the Smart Golf planning principles (especially conservation)?

What would you do?

If you decided to go for it, Smart Golf police wouldn't arrest you. You can take risks under circumstances like this when you really feel up to them. But you must be able to commit 100 percent to these higher-risk shots before going for them. As we emphasize in the next chapter: If you can't commit, don't hit. In this case, it was late in the round and your swing had felt smooth and strong all day. You realized that if you took the chance and it worked, you would really enjoy it.

If the gamble doesn't pay off, that's OK too. That happens to all golfers. You carefully considered your options, committed 100 percent to the shot, approached it with confidence and positive excitement, and went for it. You knew going in that it was not a high-percentage shot based on your current ability, but you tried. Ideally, you would just take whatever results occurred and just move on to the next shot.

Dubsdread is not a long course for PGA Tour professionals, but it challenges them as well. Without a plan, the tree-lined fairways, small greens, and numerous bunkers—over a hundred—are overwhelming; they snare even slightly wayward shots. Panic can easily set in. We mentioned earlier the fate of Greg Norman at the 1996 Masters. He met a similar ending in 1994 at Dubs. He was leading by six shots on Sunday as he made the turn. The crowds were cheering for the Shark. His adrenaline was flowing after a great front side. On the back side, he hit his driver to spots that people never knew existed. He was not in control of his mental game or his swing on that nine. He wound up losing the tournament by two shots. What happened??? He played as if he had no plan!

All golfers are subject to lapses. Fortunately ours are not as public as the professionals' or as written about as Greg Norman's. But we can all agonize with him and learn from this great player. The Smart Golf method can help you evaluate your strengths and weaknesses and plan accordingly. This can keep you in better control of your thoughts and actions.

The next chapter focuses on an element of Smart Golf, *Apply*, that can also help you control your thoughts and actions. It provides methods to increase your consistency when executing the shots that you planned. *Plan* + *Apply* = lower scores + more enjoyment.

5

Apply

If you occasionally struggle with your thoughts when you're just about to swing—or actually swinging—this chapter will help you take control. You will learn the swing thoughts of champions. You will learn about the research that explains how you perform sport skills. And you will learn the importance of your role in helping yourself find your best approach to hit a golf ball.

The *Apply* phase begins after you complete your plan for a specific shot. You have a club in your hand. You have identified a general target for the shot. Now what?

Swing Keys of Major Championship Winners

Golf Digest asked five major championship winners from 1996 something very much like this "now what?"

question. *Golf Digest* asked the champions what they thought about immediately before and during their swings. Take a look at their five sets of ideas—Table 5.1—and see if you can identify the common recommendations. In other words, what consistencies can you find in the swing keys of these five major championship winners? What differences do you find in their swing thoughts?

All five champions said they took care to focus on the target before or during their swings. For example, Tom Lehman elaborated his number one point, "get a good picture," in the following way:

> I find it difficult to play a good shot unless I know what type of shot I want to hit. That means examining my situation first. . . . Only then do I decide on a course of action.
>
> Next I visualize the shot. Before I address the ball, I see in my mind's eye the swing I want—my tempo, the ball's trajectory, spin and distance, where I want it to land, and where it's going to roll.
>
> This helps me become very target oriented. *Once I am focused on the target, I don't think of anything else* ["Swing Keys," 1997, p. 73; emphasis added].

Steve Jones, like Tom Lehman, also tries to become very target oriented before and during his swing. Jones believes "the simpler the better" helps him stay target

Table 5.1
Swing Keys of Five Major Championship Winners in 1996

Tom Lehman	Steve Jones	Annika Sorenstam
1996 British Open Champion	1996 U.S. Open Champion	1996 U.S. Women's Open Champion
1. Get a good picture.	1. Take it back smooth. A little inside. Or straight.	1. Pick your target and trust your aim.
2. Good tempo.	2. Good balance. Head still.	2. Maintain a smooth tempo throughout your swing.
3. Finish the backswing.	3. Accelerate through with back of left hand.	3. Commit 100 percent to the shot and don't worry too much about the result.
4. Start the down swing from the ground up.	4. The simpler the better.	

Mark Brooks	Nick Faldo
1996 PGA Champion	1996 Masters Champion
1. Line up club face to intermediate target.	1. Make conscious effort to start with a very slow down swing.
2. Check ball position.	2. 'Free-wheel' the driver and let it almost wrap around the neck to stop the head from coming up.
3. Take it back inside.	3. Go for a 'thump' in the bunkers, be aggressive with short follow-thru.
4. Finish the back swing.	4. When chipping, focus on a spot to read the break.
	5. Stand tall and make the arms hang when putting.

Source: From *Golf Digest.* Copyright © January 1997, pp. 72–81.

focused. "When I'm playing well, I just try to look at the target and swing." Annika Sorenstam and Mark Brooks also mentioned the importance of targets in their very first points.

Several players emphasized smoothness in their tempo or balance as a focus in their thinking. Reading between the lines a little bit, this seems like an emphasis on feel rather than mechanics. Yet mechanical thoughts appeared in every list except Annika Sorenstam's.

While these top players stressed target orientation and feel, they also varied the number of details about the swing they listed. Imagine your confusion if you combined their suggestions in one list and told yourself before every swing:

- Finish the backswing.
- Start the downswing from the ground up.
- Accelerate through with the back of the left hand.
- Take it back inside.
- Make a conscious effort to start with a very slow downswing.
- 'Free-wheel' the driver and let it almost wrap around the neck to stop the head from coming up.

These diverse mechanical thoughts actually contradict the emphasis on feel and some of the other recommendations from these same top players. How can you concentrate on target and feel at the same time as you're thinking about your left hand and your downswing? Fortunately, science has provided an answer to this dilemma. Research on sport psychology supports keeping yourself oriented to feel and target. This approach generally improves performance—especially among highly skilled and experienced athletes. We will discuss methods for doing this and related keys to effective swing thoughts later in this chapter.

Some of the other aspects of the champions' swing keys also make sense from a scientific perspective. In particular, several of them mentioned using visualization. That technique can help make the *Apply* phase work to your advantage. Finally, again reading between the lines, the champions had very specific ideas about their swing keys. We suspect they have consistent preshot routines into which these ideas fit.

This analysis suggests that five of the major champions in 1996 agreed on three ingredients worthy of inclusion in the *Apply* phase. First, they all stressed the value of focusing on the target before and during the swing. Second, "feel" is very important to them. Finally, they probably use very consistent preshot routines in order to stay very aware of their swings and make adjustments when necessary.

Now, let's take a look at ideas and techniques that can allow you to get more target and feel oriented and to use your preshot routine more consistently. We'll do this by breaking down the *Apply* phase into three components: the target phase, the preparation phase, and the execution phase.

Target Phase

The target phase moves you from a general target to a specific target. Then, through visualization or developing a feel for the target, you can commit to a specific club and specific type of shot. In other words, the three key elements of the target phase are:

- Identify a specific target.
- Use visualization or a feel for the target.
- Commit to the shot.

Identifying a Specific Target

You may recall that Figure 4.3 showed a darkened portion of the fairway of the fourteenth hole at the Winnetka Golf Club. This was the specific target suggested to the golfers in the study that we conducted on that hole. It includes an easily identifiable part of the golf course (the brightly painted 150-yard marker). That 150-yard marker served as the focal point of this specific target. A rectangular green (approximately twenty-four by twenty yards) was then envisioned around that focal point. A golfer could use this target by aiming for the middle of it.

You can also construct specific targets by using changes in coloration in the fairway, shading changes, and other landmarks. Among the landmarks that people use to construct their own temporary greens in the fairway are edges of fairway bunkers, trees, and points from which fairways bend or curve.

Why use a specific target? Some golfers argue that they have enough difficulty just hitting the fairway at all. So, the reasoning goes, it makes no sense to bother aiming for a very specific spot or even a visualized green.

Several lines of scientific research support the importance of focusing narrowly on a target during sport performance. For example, sport scientist Robert Singer and his colleagues from the University of Florida showed some advantages for targeting. In one of their studies, they used the apparatus shown in Figure 5.1. Participants used their nondominant hand (for example, right-handers used the left hand) to bounce a ball onto a target approximately ten feet away. One group, the "awareness" group, was instructed to focus on the way they threw the ball at the target and to pay attention to specific cues, such as the feeling of the movement and the noise of the ball hitting the target. In other words, this awareness group focused on some mechanical aspects of throwing. A second group, the "non-awareness" group, focused simply on the target itself. They were advised to focus on the center of the target and to ignore information about how their hands moved or other aspects of the situation. They were instructed to let the throwing movement flow and to perform the task as automatically as possible.

The "non-awareness" group (or target-focused group) performed far better than the awareness group. That is, focusing on the target produced more accurate throwing than focusing on some mechanical aspects of throwing the ball. While this shows the importance of target focusing, however, it does not prove that using mechanical swing thoughts will ruin your golf swing. The mechanical thoughts used by subjects in Singer's awareness group may simply not have been the *right* mechanical thoughts for that task. We don't know if it improves ball throwing with our nondominant hands to focus on the feel of the ball or the noise the ball makes when it hits the target. In contrast, when Steve Jones tells himself to "accelerate through with the back of left hand," that swing mechanic probably improves the efficiency of his swing. So if you use mechanical swing thoughts, don't try to abandon them just because of this research. Just make sure your mechanically oriented swing thoughts actually improve the efficiency of your swing. Irrelevant mechanics may hinder your swing, highly relevant ones may not. Also, use the

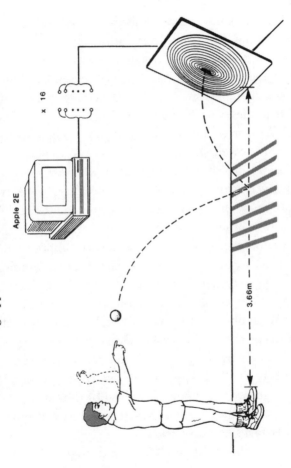

Figure 5.1
Ball-Throwing Apparatus and a Subject at the Throwing Line

Apple 2E

x 16

3.66m

Source: Reprinted by permission from R. N. Singer, R. Lidor, and J. H. Cauraugh, 1993, "To Be Aware or Not Aware? What to Think About While Learning and Performing a Motor Skill," *The Sport Psychologist,* Vol. 7 (No.1), p. 24.

Singer research to remember the importance of focusing on the target.

Researchers have also found that expert performers often show heart rate deceleration as they execute the skills in their sports. Archers, rifle-shooters, and golfers have shown this pattern. For example, sport psychologist Stephen Boutcher (a former highly ranked amateur golfer from Scotland) and his colleague Nathaniel Zinsser found that elite golfers, compared to beginners, showed slower heart rates immediately before, during, and after striking the ball while attempting to sink twelve-foot putts. Such deceleration of heart rates can cause changes in electrical activity in the brain that improve ability to focus attention on a target.

Yet another line of scientific evidence supports the importance of focusing on your specific target in golf. Do you think it helps you to get feedback on different aspects of your golf swing from a teaching professional? What about the effects of watching the flight of your shots on the driving range? Do both of these types of feedback always help you swing better? Do they help you 90 percent, 80 percent, or 50 percent of the time? Research shows that about one-third of the time, performance actually gets *worse* when performers of sport and other tasks get feedback.

Psychologists Avraham Kluger and Angelo De Nise attempted to explain this surprising finding. They discovered that feedback that keeps attention focused on the task often produces positive results. Feedback that is too negative or focused on the characteristics of the person can have negative effects on performance. So, if your golf instructor (or friend acting as a teacher) keeps telling you what you're doing wrong, that feedback could actually worsen your swing. Focusing on what you are doing well and on the task at hand improves performance far better than negative feedback.

These conclusions support Smart Golf's emphasis on positive focusing. They also suggest finding a way to stay task oriented. One method of doing this is to focus on the specific target very deliberately.

Using Imagery

I think you have to rehearse in your mind, over and over again, the event before it happens. That's exactly what I did before the final round of the U.S. Open in 1993. I rehearsed every shot several times before I went to the first tee with a one shot lead over some of the best golfers in the history of the game. Roger Bannister, when he broke the 4-minute mile, it had never been done in the history of time. He rehearsed it in his mind, over and over, hundreds of times before he ever did it. That's why he did it. Emotionally, he did it. That's the whole thing; 37 people broke it after him, that same year. Nobody in the history of time until he did and then 37 people right after him. That shows you how we hold ourselves back with our beliefs [Lee Janzen, quoted in Hanley, 1994].

Both Tom Lehman, the 1996 PGA Player of the Year and Vardon Trophy winner, and Lee Janzen, the 1993 U.S. Open Champion, are big believers in using imagery to improve their performances. Janzen didn't quite get the facts right about what happened after Roger Bannister broke the four-minute mile. Janzen thought thirty-seven men broke that amazing record in 1954 after Bannister showed them the way. Actually, only four other men broke the four-minute mile in 1954 after Bannister did it. But this was a record that knowledgeable people argued could *never* be broken. In fact, at least fifty articles in medical journals prior to 1954 drew that conclusion.

Surveys of elite athletes show that approximately 90 percent agree with Janzen and Lehman about the importance of using imagery in sport performance. These elite athletes use imagery to practice skills and strategies, to recall and control emotions, to improve concentration, and to set goals. Research on the effectiveness of imagery shows that the technique can improve performance in basketball, football, swimming, dart throwing, alpine skiing, karate, volleyball serving, tennis serving, weight lifting, muscular endurance, distance running, gymnastics, figure skating, and—last but not least—golf.

Imagery works its magic by establishing mental blueprints. These blueprints can trigger your muscles to respond to the stimulus aspects of the task. For example, as you imagine taking the club back during your golf swing, the muscles in your arms and back develop a more automatic way of responding to the image of moving away from the ball. Stimuli such as the sight of the ball and the sight of the hands and arms moving away from the ball become cues for the muscles to activate. Visualization lets you form images of these stimuli for yourself—so you can practice without having to pay for buckets of balls.

Great Images: Vividness and Controllability

The best images are vivid and controllable. Vivid images include a great deal of detail about the environment. They include the sights, sounds, smells, and textures of the setting in which you participate. Vivid images also contain details about the emotions and thoughts that you experience while you play golf. An extremely vivid image of an attempt to make a five-foot putt to win a match would include, for example, some degree of anxiety or tension, perhaps some chatter with a partner, and the feeling of intense concentration immediately before beginning a preputt routine.

Great images are also controllable. You want images in which you are in control of your golf swing and the flight of the ball. You want to see the ball do what you intend it to do in these images. This means that you want to see images of the ball rolling into the cup after you hit it during your mental putt. If you are a righty and want the ball to draw, your image should show the ball drawing toward the target and then landing on your specific target.

Following are several imagery exercises. These exercises can help you improve the vividness and controllability of your images. Take a few minutes to try the exercises for yourself.

Improving the Vividness and Controllability of Images

Vividness

Try these exercises to develop your ability to re-create richly vivid images of the world around you.

- *A room in your home or office.* Imagine your room for a few moments. Place yourself in a familiar chair. Look around and take in all the details. What do you see? What are the shapes and textures of the objects in front of you? What sounds do you hear? Can you hear noises or conversations outside your door? Can you sense any movements outside your room? What are you smelling? Try to use all your senses and take it all in.

  The next time you are in the room, redo this exercise. Go to the chair and sit in it. Close your eyes and recreate the images in front of you. Open your eyes and see what details you can add to the images. Be sure to focus on the sights, sounds, and feel of it.

- *The first hole at a familiar course.* What can you recall about the first hole of this familiar course? What do you see in front of you as you stare down the fairway? What does the grass look like? Smell like? Can you see distinctions between the fairway and the rough? What do the trees look like? How many trees and bushes can you re-create in your mind's eye? What are the shapes of the hazards and the contours of the fairway? What does the ground feel like under your feet? What colors do you see? What sounds do you hear?

The next time you are at this course, redo this exercise. Stand on the first tee for a few moments and close your eyes. Just imagine what is in front of you and then open your eyes and add details about the sights, sounds, smells, and feel that appear before you.

Controllability

Making the images as vivid as you can, try these exercises to develop your ability to picture things happening just as you wish them to.

• *A difficult putt.* Imagine a difficult putt at a familiar course. Pick a putt that either has a good deal of break to it or is particularly fast or particularly slow. Then imagine yourself going through your entire preputt routine. This could include identifying an intermediate target or a target line. It could include crouching down to see the line and observe the contours of the green. Just include whatever you do to take practice strokes and prepare yourself for hitting the shot. Then, see yourself standing above the ball and stroking it solidly. Imagine the feel of the ball coming off the putting head. Imagine the ball rolling, rolling, rolling, taking the bend in the green as you had hoped it would and falling directly into the middle of the cup. Can you hear the sound the ball makes when it clangs into the bottom of the cup?

• *Recovering from a mistake in a friendly round.* Imagine missing a three-foot putt during a friendly round.

Can you recreate how you would feel and what your reaction would be? Can you develop a reaction that would allow you to experience the disappointment and then begin to move on to the next shot? Try to recreate the feeling of the moment as it would have occurred. Take the feeling of disappointment, anger, or frustration and find a way of turning it into a positive focus on the task at hand. Can you tell yourself that everyone misses some of them some of the time? Can you see yourself making some correction in the stroke that could prevent the problem the next time around? Can you see yourself moving on from there with a positive attitude toward the next shot? Try to redirect your attention in the image from the disappointment and frustration to an optimistic focus on the next target.

• *Recovering from a mistake in a competitive round.* Imagine missing a three-foot putt during an intensely competitive round. This could be a weekend match that you play with a regular partner against another team. It could be a tournament in which you participate individually or as a team member. Would your reaction to this short missed putt differ from your reaction to a similar miss in a friendly round? How would you feel about disappointing your teammate? Can you see yourself turning the frustration around? (Try *not* to picture yourself apologizing. In a real game you'd need to talk this over with your teammate beforehand, of course, but we've found that teams play better if they adopt the following rule: *No apologies to each other; you both agree to do the best you can on every shot—so there can't be anything to apologize for.*) Can you see yourself accept the missed putt as something that happens to everyone—especially those who don't practice putting for an hour or two each day? Can you make a slight correction in your alignment or stroke, take a rehearsal swing, and move on from there? Try to redirect your attention in the image from frustration to optimism.

Feel for the Target

Many people are more feel oriented than visually oriented. Feel orientation helps golfers develop a keen awareness of the movements in golf. They feel the pace of their swings and the length of their swings for certain types of shots. Their practice swings help them literally rehearse the feel they intend to use for the forthcoming shots. They take this rehearsal of the feel and translate it into a *kinesthetic* (movement) image. With these individuals, the target phase works best by using kinesthetic images to get a feel for how the shot will get to the target.

Consider the feel developed by the winner of the 1904 British Amateur Championship late in the competition: "The first ball I struck I knew I was on the road to recovery. For the first time in two weeks I could feel the ball. The necessary touch and the resultant timing were there in sharp contradistinction to the entire absence of these vitally important essentials previously, that I was at once transported in to the golfer's seventh heaven of delight" (Travis, 1910).

Gary McCord and Peter Kostis (1996), two well-known golf teachers and commentators, recently described a lesson that they gave to a PGA tour player to help him develop more of a feel for his swing. They had this golfer play four holes starting at 10 P.M. They suggested to the golfer that he "just get up and 'feel' the ball down the darkened corridor. You must feel your swing and what kind of shot it produced if you are going to find the ball. Hit it, feel it, and listen to it. This is the call of night golf."

McCord and Kostis described the approach as one that can help a golfer avoid "thinking of seventeen positions during a swing." It might help golfers play without focusing excessively on technique, perhaps decreasing panic about the position of the clubface. It could let them just hit the ball with more confidence that it will go where it's supposed to go. McCord and Kostis view this as a method of avoiding "golf overload." You might want to try this to see if you respond with better feel after listening to the "call of night golf."

Committing to the Shot

Annika Sorenstam sums up this issue by saying, "Commit 100 percent and don't worry about the result. What the ball does after it leaves the clubface is beyond my control. I try to be in the right frame of mind and hit each shot as best I can. If I achieve that goal and the result is poor, there is no point worrying. I accept the outcome and disassociate things I can control with the things I cannot" ("Swing Keys," 1997, p. 77).

Annika Sorenstam knows that when she does not commit to the shot she plans to hit, the odds of a mishit go way up. Have you had that experience? Let's say that you are in between an 8-iron and 7-iron on an approach to a particular green. You decide on an easy 7, but doubt lingers as you approach the ball. As you begin to swing, the cloud of doubt becomes darker and darker. As you swing in that cloud, you notice your choppy backswing and proceed to hit a chubby 7-iron. *If you can't commit, don't hit!*

Commitment and Success

A strong commitment to a shot results in a clearer image of it and better execution of the desired shot. If your commitment waffles, step back for a second and image the shot again. See or feel yourself hitting it with the club that you selected. Make sure that you can imagine a positive outcome for the club (and shot) you selected. If—for whatever reason—you can't believe in a positive outcome, select another club or another kind of shot.

Commitment promotes positive expectations. When you commit to a shot, you expect it to go well. If you expect to do well, you can commit. This notion lies at the very heart of the philosophy of the head coach of the Swedish Golf Federation, Pia Nilsson. Nilsson coached Annika Sorenstam and Liselotte Neumann, clearly two of the best women golfers in the world today. Among the truths about golf that Nilsson preaches are:

- To play eighteen holes in fifty-four strokes is possible.
- Human beings are always more important than their performances.
- Human beings have unlimited potential.
- Each human being is unique.

Certainly Nilsson advises her players to *expect* to play well. In the spring of 1996, for example, Nilsson encouraged the notoriously shy young Swede, Sophie Gustafson, to stand up in a workshop and make a winner's speech. The terrified Gustafson managed a smile and said, "Thank you!" A group of her peers and coaches applauded enthusiastically. Nilsson specifically encouraged Gustafson and reassured her that her speech was just fine. After showing a great deal of promise without winning anything, Gustafson went out following this workshop and immediately won a Swedish tour event. A month later she won her first European-tour event at the Swiss Open.

Positive expectations can work as long as you stay within a reasonable boundary of reality. You will recall our elaborate discussion of the dangers of positive illusions in Chapter Four. You want to expect and believe that you can hit the shot you are intending to hit. However, the plan that you create must be bounded by the reality of your current skill level. If you follow that guideline, then you can stay very positive. In other words, positive illusions should not hurt you when you get to this stage of performance. They can hinder you in the *Plan* phase (a lot!), but not in the *Apply* phase.

Mind over Muscle

The power of positive expectations deserves further elaboration. Twenty-four men were once tested for arm strength (Nelson and Furst, 1972). These men were also asked to rate their strength compared to each of the other twenty-three men in the study. Subjects were then paired and asked to arm wrestle each other. The researchers arranged the pairs so that one man was clearly stronger than the other. However, both men believed that the stronger man was actually the weaker. So, the objectively stronger men *expected* to lose to the weaker men. Ten of the twelve contests (83 percent) were won by the man who tested weaker! These results suggest that expectations can overcome physical strength.

Expectations can powerfully influence perceptions and behavior. You want to harness this power to help you commit 100 percent to each shot immediately before swinging the club. You want to expect to hit the shot you are about to try at that moment. In the *Plan* phase you want to keep your expectations bounded by the realities of the situation you face. This means taking care to use the planning principles (such as conservation and personal par) to keep your expectations realistic. Then, when you get to the Apply phase, you want to become as positive as you can be. Remember, *if you can't commit, don't hit.* Before swinging, find a shot you can really believe in.

Preparation Phase

The preparation phase begins with a strong commitment to a specific shot and ends when you start the backswing. The primary purpose of this phase is to help you develop a very consistent preshot routine and focus very carefully on alignment.

Preshot Routine

Try to identify your preshot routines for executing both a putt and a full shot. How do you approach the ball? How do you include alignment and target focusing? Do you take rehearsal swings? If so, where do you swing relative to the address position and how many swings do you take?

Many golfers say that they can identify their pre-putt routines much more easily than their preswing routines. The simpler motion (fewer moving parts) required for putting makes it easier to focus on preparation before the putt. The longer swing motion of the full swing requires more timing and sequencing; this, in turn, draws attention to the mechanical aspects of the swing. Focusing on mechanics can decrease attention to the preshot routine.

Preshot Routines of Expert Golfers

Expert golfers show a great deal of consistency in their preshot routines. In fact, two sport psychologists who themselves are expert golfers, Debra Crews and Stephen Boutcher (1986, p. 55), found many commonalties among the preshot routines of twelve LPGA players whom they observed very carefully:

Full Swing Preshot Routine

1. Stand behind the ball.
2. Move beside the ball.
3. Set the club behind the ball with one glance at the target.
4. Set the feet.
5. Use a combination of three waggles with two glances toward the target.
6. Swing.

Putting Preshot Routine

1. Stand behind the ball.
2. Move beside the ball.
3. Take two practice swings.
4. Set the club behind the ball with one glance at the target.
5. Set the feet.

6. Take two glances at the target.

7. Putt.

The researchers noticed some differences between the full swing routines and the putting routines. For example, only two of the twelve players used a practice swing for the full swing, whereas nine of them used at least one practice stroke in their putting routines. You can also see the very clear emphasis on alignment in both full swing and putting routines. The golfers generally stood behind the ball (apparently to identify a target line and an intermediate target) before addressing the ball. They also took care to set the club behind the ball to ensure club-to-target alignment before setting the feet in position. Crews and Boutcher also found that the better golfers took a bit longer for their preshot routines. This reflected a greater degree of consistency and deliberateness in the preshot routines of the better players.

How does your preshot routine compare with those of the LPGA players described here? You may notice yourself using more rehearsal swings, for example. You may also notice that you had a difficult time even identifying the nature of your preshot routine, particularly for your full swing. Have you noticed that some touring pros, like Lee Trevino and Greg Norman, perform their preshot routines rather quickly? Others, such as Jack Nicklaus, Tom Kite, and Betsy King, are far more deliberate in their preshot routines. The pace of your preshot routine may match one or another of these players. A purposeful routine with consistency, not pace per se, is the key.

Advantages of Preshot Routines

Golfers wait a long time between shots. After you hit a shot, you have to walk or ride to get to the ball—and oftentimes wait your turn to hit the next shot. This could take several minutes. Other sports—tennis, for example—involve much less time between opportunities to hit. The extraordinary length of time in golf compared to other sports leaves room for golfers to become distracted by their own thoughts or by something happening to other players. A very consistent preshot routine can help you channel your attention into the task before you. It gives you a way to spend a few seconds or more warming up to the kind of shot you want to hit and getting oriented to your target. If you went from shot to shot without a consistent preshot routine in place, you would find yourself changing your tempo dramatically and sometimes neglecting some key aspects of preparation (such as a consistent set-up and alignment).

Another major advantage of preshot routines are that they help the golf swing become more automatic. This frees up energy and attention from the mechanical aspects.

Emphasis on Alignment

The best golfer of the past decade, Greg Norman, attributed his ability to sink a critical putt in a recent tournament to the use of a great intermediate target. Norman sank a fairly straight fifteen-footer on the final hole of his thirty-six-hole match with Scott Hoch to win the $1 million first prize in the 1997 Andersen Consulting World Championship of Golf. You may not (OK, will not) get a chance to make a putt for a million dollars. But you can learn to find your own great spots on every shot you attempt.

You can see that all discussions of preshot routines emphasize alignment. Very small errors in alignment can produce huge problems in direction. For this reason, some of the best players in the world, including Mark Brooks (see Table 5.1), very explicitly remind themselves to align the shot every single time. You can use an alignment routine to provide that reminder as well. If you establish a routine that includes consistent alignment, you won't ever feel comfortable hitting a shot without going through that routine. You may have noticed this type of feeling regarding seat belts. After you got used to using seat belts, you probably began to feel uncomfortable driving without them. That's the feeling you want to encourage for every shot before swinging.

An alignment routine includes the following elements:

1. *Target line.* Determine a straight line to the target from behind the ball. Ten out of Crews and Boutcher's twelve LPGA players started their preshot routines for full swings by standing behind the ball. Eleven of them started behind the ball for their preputt routines. All amateurs would be well advised to start behind the ball to identify their target line. When you stand directly behind the ball in line with your target, you can create an imaginary line between your ball and the target.

2. *Intermediate target.* Many players find an intermediate target two to four feet in front of the ball directly on the target line. You can use a divot, a distinctive blade of grass, or a twig to identify this intermediate target. The more distinctive the intermediate target, the better it is. It's critical to identify this intermediate target while you're standing behind the ball. Then you can move to the side of the ball and still see that great intermediate target. This intermediate target is much easier to see and use for club and body alignment than the more distant specific target. When you turn to see a distant target to align the club and your body, you can lose consistency of alignment. The amount of rotation of your head and body to see the target varies with the distance from the target and thus influences how the club is aligned to the target.

3. *Club alignment.* Grip the club either in your nondominant hand or in both hands. You can do this from behind the ball while you're still looking at the intermediate target or from the side of the ball, parallel to your target line. Get in the address position and then align the club to the intermediate target.

4. *Body alignment.* Now align your body to the club. Once your body is aligned to your club, set your posture.

This alignment element of preparation to hit a golf ball is among the more difficult things to master. Most golfers could use help from a qualified teaching professional to develop a consistent procedure for alignment. Golfers often have difficulty getting the notion of alignment and a routine for consistency. These critical qualities of the Apply phase are often taken for granted.

This applies to all golfers, including one of the most talented and controversial players in recent years—John Daly, winner of the 1991 PGA championship and the 1995 British Open. Daly, the longest hitter on the PGA tour before Tiger Woods joined the tour, had only one top ten finish in 1996. More recently, he finished in the top ten at the 1997 Bob Hope Chrysler Classic. In interviews after the tournament, Daly noted that he had watched videos of his best tournaments. He discovered that the squareness of his alignment when putting was much better in those days. With the help of an experienced teaching professional, he was able to improve his alignment considerably.

Focusing on alignment should be the foundation for every shot you hit. You can own this aspect of *Apply* and consistently check for consistency. This approach allows you to begin focusing for the thirty to forty-five seconds that it takes for you to hit a shot. It puts you into your own little world. Take time to get this control.

To develop your routine further, watch the professional golfers on television very carefully. Watch their preshot routines. Note similarities and differences among these players. Take notes on the players. Use the routines of experts presented following as a guide. Some players are very methodical, others are more flowing. You may identify with a player who matches your style. Let your personality and disposition direct you.

Changing Toward the Expert Stage

These three exercises will help you refine your swing and make yourself more of an expert golfer.

- *Two-station practicing.* Establish two stations when you practice. One is a technique station with an alignment club on the ground. The second is a target station. In the technique station, give yourself permission to think mechanics and work on swing improvements. Work on only one part at a time: two practice swings to one ball hit. Hit only five balls (maximum) and then move to the target station. In the target station, work on the transition to the target mode. Use three swings with different targets and different clubs. If you are not ready to focus exclusively on the target, work on your swing keys. The closer you can get to pure target focusing, the smoother and more automatic your swing will be.

- *Blind swings.* Make practice swings with your eyes shut to feel the movement. Then make swings with your eyes open trying to match your practice swings. Practicing putting with your eyes shut can establish real trust in your motion.

- *Old versus new in the mirror.* Make a swing with your old swing, then with the desired change to concentrate on the differences in the feeling between the two. Use a mirror to see the differences. Try to match the feel with what you see.

Another way to refine your routine involves practicing with a friend. On the range, identify a target and your desired ball flight. Go through your preshot routine five or six times to different targets. Have a friend jot down your sequence and note the accuracy of your alignment. How does your routine compare with the routine outlined previously? Is there an area of inconsistency that your friend observed? How consistent is your alignment? It is hard to see yourself. Our intentions and actions often differ more than we think. The feedback from a friend can help you make some constructive changes in this regard.

Execution Phase

This phase begins with the initiation of the swing motion and ends with the completion of the swing. It raises the question of what to think about as you swing. At this point, we know that focusing on the target can prove very helpful, especially for advanced players. Let's consider again whether mechanically oriented swing thoughts are OK for some golfers, some of the time. For example, can it help you to think "make a full pivot" or "extend and through" or "big finish"?

Target Focusing With or Without Swing Thoughts

We have discussed the many advantages of focusing on the target. This target focusing occurs through visual imagery or kinesthetic imagery. As you waggle the club and get comfortable over it, you could use your feeling for the target at this point. You may recall the earlier discussion of the research by Singer and associates on awareness when executing sport performance. Singer's findings suggested the importance of focusing on the target instead of focusing on mechanical aspects of the swing. Remember that Singer had his subjects use their nondominant hands in a novel task (bouncing a ball into a target). Researcher Barry Zimmerman and his colleagues studied a more familiar though still difficult task—throwing darts.

Dart throwing shares some similarities with golf. In both sports, experts generally agree about the methods of execution that produce the best outcomes. When Zimmerman and his colleagues taught their subjects to throw darts, they relied on a long history of dart throwing and well-developed knowledge about what it takes to throw darts most effectively. They had their subjects look and listen to a videotaped set of instructions that took them through the grip, the stance, and the process of sighting (focusing on the target), throwing, and following through. Each of these five aspects of throwing darts had very specific directions.

Zimmerman and his associates found that when subjects used a "dynamic cue," they performed better than when they used a "fixed cue." The fixed cue was very much like Singer's target-focused ("non-aware") approach. This group simply focused on the bull's-eye and tried to throw the dart to it. In contrast, the "dynamic cue" subjects focused on their forearm positions and their follow-through motions. They used these as "throw thoughts" just as many golfers focus on their shoulder turns or take-aways and follow-throughs as swing thoughts. Although the "dynamic cue" group's success may seem surprising in light of the Singer study, remember that Zimmerman's dart throwers did receive useful suggestions about throw thoughts that could help them throw darts more accurately.

Zimmerman's research suggests that swing thoughts can help, but Singer's suggests such thoughts don't help. At first glance, this leaves golfers who like to use swing thoughts in a dilemma. Whose results should they use? Should they try to rid their minds of swing thoughts or use them?

You can resolve this dilemma by realizing that Singer's swing thought group ("awareness") received general directions about becoming aware of the feeling of the ball leaving the hand and the sound that the ball makes when it hits the target. Awareness of these factors probably had very little beneficial impact on the performance of that task. Awareness of the target, however, did prove much more effective than no instructions at all. Zimmerman's "effective throw thought" subjects used mechanical thoughts that are known to be useful when throwing darts.

Effective Swing Thoughts

In golf, swing thoughts that relate to positions, such as where your hands are at the top of the swing, tend to inhibit the overall smoothness of the swing motion. However, when you try to change your swing or learn a new shot, conscious thought is necessary until you can perform the movement consistently. The goal is to move from thought mode to target mode as quickly as possible. You may read or hear teachers say, "just let it go" or "just think target." You can't "let go" of what you don't have!

Figure 5.2 shows a continuum from the beginning stages of learning to the expert stage. Beginners use deliberate learning strategies, emphasizing mechanics. Experts focus on targets and execute with more automatic and less deliberate processing. The shaded area in the middle shows the transition stage. When you are in the transition stage, some of the time you attempt to execute a new shot or new swing element, it works; some of the time, it doesn't. You won't jump from learning to automatic processing overnight, nor will you be able to take a change immediately to the course. Through effective practice and repetition, the movement you seek will become more habitual. Changing Toward the Expert Stage provides exercises to help you work through changes and to practice the *Apply* phase on the practice range.

You may reach the expert stage and still want a swing key. That's fine. Use keys that emphasize the

Figure 5.2
The Transition from Beginner to Expert in Golf

BEGINNER
LEARNING
MECHANICS

TRANSITION

EXPERT
AUTOMATIC
TARGET

whole swing, not specific parts of it. As Gene Sarazen (1950) put it, "[ambitious players] mustn't destroy [their] concentration before a shot by wondering if 33 anatomical parts are going to perform their appointed functions." Some simple whole thoughts are "stretch and spring," "back and through," and "hello—Dolly." The swing keys need to have meaning to the user—not necessarily anyone else. Your keys may change. Keep a notebook of keys that work or feelings that you can go back and recapture.

The target, preparation, and execution components of the *Apply* phase can help you identify a specific target, use imagery to your advantage, commit 100 percent to the shot, establish a very consistent preshot routine that emphasizes careful alignment, and execute your swings with clear focus on the target and—if needed—whole swing thoughts. Major championship winners take care to focus on specific targets and keep their preshot routines consistent. Players at the elite level also emphasize the importance of their kinesthetic (feel-oriented) focusing and images. You can work toward developing your skills so that feel and target focusing become your swing keys. You will need lots of deliberate thoughts (conscious control) and practice to make the transition from focusing on components of your swing to the more automatic, feel- and target-oriented approach used by expert golfers. Meanwhile, as you make the transition to the target mode, keep your swing thoughts whole ("back and through") to encourage a smooth, efficient motion.

The next chapter focuses on *React*. If you can keep your reactions calm and positive, you can follow your *Plan* and maintain an effective and consistent *Apply* phase. If your reactions get negative and distracting, you will diffuse your focus on your plan and your approach to and through the ball. This will compromise both your score and your enjoyment of the game.

6

React and the 4-F Technique

 One of Bobby Jones's contemporaries and certainly one of the best golfers in the United States in the 1920s and 1930s was "Light Horse" Harry Cooper. Light Horse Harry got his name because of the speed with which he played his shots and chased after them, according to writer Herbert Warren Wind. Apparently, Light Horse Harry was a happy extrovert who bubbled with confident conversation and loved the attention of the galleries.

Harry Cooper's confidence turned sour when he came within two inches of winning the U.S. Open in 1927. He had an eight-foot downhill putt for birdie on the seventy-first hole. He ran it four feet by. Observers said he looked extremely serious, not bubbly at all, when he lined up that four-footer. He missed.

By the end of the third round of the 1936 U.S. Open, it finally looked like the Light Horse was going to get his crown. Professional golfers played thirty-six holes to end the U.S. Open in those days. After the first eighteen gave Harry Cooper a two-stroke lead, he looked "fidgety" and "anxious." Those who followed him that fateful day could "almost feel the terrific nervous strain under which Cooper was playing" (Wind, 1956, p. 361).

Unfortunately, the Light Horse struggled after making birdie on the eighth hole of the final round. He bogeyed the fourteenth, fifteenth, and eighteenth. Still, he had played well enough to shoot a 73 and felt fairly certain that his 284 total (a new U.S. Open record at the time) could not be beaten. Sadly for Light Horse Harry, a relatively unknown pro named Tony Manero took a three on the eighteenth hole—which compared very favorably to the five that Harry had taken earlier in the day. Manero's 282 meant that Light Horse Harry Cooper was a champion whose name was never inscribed among America's national champions.

This "Tragedy of Harry Cooper" (as Wind called it in 1956) suggests that some troubling emotions caused Light Horse Harry Cooper's failure to win a national title. He was a happy, bubbly, confident extrovert. Yet worry, regret, somberness, and anxiety contributed to his failures during the waning moments of the two U.S. Opens that he almost won.

We cannot know for sure whether emotions in fact derailed the Light Horse. Yet we know that emotions can lead to disaster on the golf course when those emotions are very negative. And we know that positive emotions can maximize performance for most players most of the time.

This chapter will help you understand how emotions can affect your golf game and how to harness them to help lower your scores and improve your enjoyment. After considering dimensions of emotion, we review the manner in which emotions affect sport performance. This review focuses on a recent, interesting, and very useful theory called the Zone of Optimal Functioning (ZOF). The third and final section of the chapter discusses how to find your ZOF and keep yourself there.

 ## Dimensions of Emotion

The most important thing for golfers of all ages and handicaps is not that they should play golf well, but that they should play it cheerfully. One wonders why some people choose to play a game at all which apparently gives them about [four] hours of complete misery. A habit of being irritable at golf grows upon a man without his knowing it, until at length he is a burden to his partner, opponent, caddie, and most of all to himself. . . . If you realize at the beginning that to be a good golfer you must, before all things, control your temper, you will find after awhile that it is just as easy to be cheerful as not and a great deal more pleasant. And the result of this schooling of the temper is that you are a better and more lovable person in all relations of life [Whigham, 1910/1986, p. 181].

Is Whigham right? Certainly it is a great deal more pleasant to be cheerful than to be angry and morose. He may not be right when he says, "you will find after awhile that it is just as easy to be cheerful as not." For many golfers, being cheerful on the golf course is anything but easy.

Before we consider how best to "school your temper" in golf, we need a common language to describe emotions. Whigham, for example, used such terms as irritability, complete misery, angry, and morose. Are these emotions the same or similar or quite different? Take a few minutes and complete the following exercise to clarify the meaning of words that are commonly used to describe emotions.

Dimensions of Emotions

The following list contains words that describe different kinds of moods and feelings. Review each word and consider which of them describe how you feel *now*. Then think about which words describe how you felt during the final holes of your last round of golf.

Right Now	Playing Golf	Emotion
_____	_____	afraid
_____	_____	alarmed
_____	_____	angry
_____	_____	annoyed
_____	_____	aroused
_____	_____	astonished
_____	_____	bored
_____	_____	calm
_____	_____	content
_____	_____	delighted
_____	_____	depressed
_____	_____	distressed
_____	_____	droopy
_____	_____	excited
_____	_____	frustrated
_____	_____	glad
_____	_____	gloomy
_____	_____	happy
_____	_____	miserable
_____	_____	pleased
_____	_____	relaxed
_____	_____	sad
_____	_____	satisfied
_____	_____	serene
_____	_____	sleepy
_____	_____	tense
_____	_____	tired

How would you describe the differences or the similarities
in the emotions you indicated for your present state (now)

> compared to the state you recalled from your last round of golf? Can you identify dimensions of moods or emotions from this list of words?

The exercise features twenty-seven words out of the huge English vocabulary for emotion. It could have presented many other words, such as *affectionate, agitated, aggressive, alone, amused, awful, blue, cool, desperate, discouraged, disgusted, enraged, free, good, hostile, indignant, interested, jealous, lost, mean, nervous, panicky, reckless, rejected, secure, steady, sullen, sympathetic, tender, tormented, warm,* and *wild.* These and other emotions differ in shades of meaning from the ones shown. Yet research from the past forty years shows that the twenty-seven words listed capture the most common and distinctive emotional states.

Figure 6.1 shows the dimensions that James Russell (1980) found particularly useful when defining emotional states. He noted that emotions vary in intensity, from high to low. Emotions also, more obviously, vary in valence from positive to negative.

In each of the four quadrants of Figure 6.1, you can see a particular emotion that captures the essence of that quadrant. For example, in the upper left quadrant, the one characterized by both positive and high-intensity emotions, the term *excited* appears in a box. An excited state is moderately high in intensity and rather positive in overall impact for most people. In a similar vein, the

**Figure 6.1
The Wheel of Emotions.**

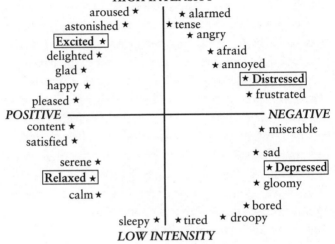

Source: Russell, J. A. (1980). A circumplex model of affect. *Journal of Personality and Social Psychology, 39,* 1161–1178. Copyright © 1980 by the American Psychological Association. Adapted with permission.

quadrant labeled *depressed* represents an extremely negative state that is moderately low in intensity. *Relaxed* captures a positive low-intensity mood and *distressed* captures a negative high-intensity mood.

Using a variety of statistical techniques, Russell (and others) have actually rated where each of these words belongs on the tone and intensity dimensions.

Figure 6.1 includes locations for each word on those dimensions. You can see that most people consider the word *tense* to be rather high in intensity, but also quite neutral in tone. You could feel tense in a positive and excited way. You could also feel tense in a negative or nervous way. By contrast, *frustrated* is a largely negative mood to most people and one that is only moderately high in intensity. You can also see that words like *sleepy* and *tired* capture very low-intensity feelings that are also rather neutral in tone. Sometimes feeling sleepy can be a rather positive state while other times it can be somewhat negative. Perhaps much of the time, most of us simply accept our tiredness or sleepiness as a part of living and don't put a lot of positive or negative meaning into those states. *Droopy* captures a tired state that feels more negative for most people.

This common language for emotional states will allow you to understand your golf game more completely. You will see that each of us has an emotional zone, located somewhere on Figure 6.1, that helps us perform particularly well.

Finding Your Zone of Optimal Functioning

Psychologist Uri Hanin (1980) suggested that each individual has an emotional state that helps set the stage for an optimal level of performance. Some individuals perform best when they feel fairly tense. Others perform best when more relaxed. Hanin defined the emotional state associated with maximum performance as the Zone of Optimal Functioning (ZOF). Recent research with pistol shooters and soccer players supports the ZOF idea. Evaluations of emotional states were taken with these athletes before many competitions. Then the emotional states of the athletes before their best performances were compared with their emotional states before their worst performances. The emotions associated with the best performances defined their individual ZOFs. When the athletes felt emotionally out of their ZOFs, their performances were poorer than their ZOF performances.

You can identify your own ZOF by carefully studying your best performances. You can complete the "how do you feel now" side of the previous exercise prior to each round of golf. After ten to twenty rounds of golf, you can compare your better rounds with your worst rounds. You may note that you performed better when feeling more intensity than you expected. Or you may find that you performed best when you were in a more serene or relaxed state.

Figure 6.2 shows our rough estimates of the ZOFs of fourteen well-known touring pros. Our views by no means represent objective reality. They simply reflect our impressions at the moment. How would your placements of these players in Figure 6.2 compare with ours? We suspect you will agree on some of the major points. For example, most of the golfers whom we've asked to review this figure place almost all the players on the positive side of the diagram. Also, more players appear toward the excited quadrant than any of the three other quadrants.

Notice also the range of ZOFs among these world-class players. Azinger and Trevino simply function at their best with different moods than people like Soren-

Figure 6.2
ZOFs for Fourteen Elite Golfers

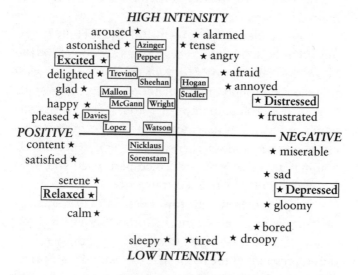

Source: Russell, J. A. (1980). A circumplex model of affect. *Journal of Personality and Social Psychology, 39,* 1161–1178. Copyright © 1980 by the American Psychological Association. Adapted with permission.

stam and Nicklaus. Golfers like Craig Stadler and Ben Hogan (from a different era) have played magnificent golf despite maintaining a certain negativity in their emotional styles.

Figure 6.2 suggests that most elite golfers' ZOFs are positive and neutral to moderate in intensity. Figure 6.3 provides a useful way of describing more completely the range of ZOFs that are quite effective for golfers. The shaded areas indicate an Excited ZOF (top), a Relaxed ZOF (bottom), and a Moderately Intense Positive ZOF (middle). Which one, if any, describes your ZOF?

Unfortunately, the inherent difficulty of the game of golf pulls golfers in a negative emotional direction. When the ball flies into the woods, it is rather dramatic. The sound of the ball clattering through the branches as it disappears from view tends to stick in one's memory. Golfers also have several minutes before getting to do anything active after one of these dramatically negative moments. As we've discussed before, most other sports allow for some immediate distractions after a poor play or shot, but golf does not. This makes golf perhaps the most challenging game from an emotional perspective.

Why Negativity Creates Problems for Golfers

Negativity poses special problems for sport participants, including golfers. Negative events elicit more biological, emotional, intellectual, and behavioral activity than

Figure 6.3
Excited, Relaxed, and Moderately Intense Positive ZOFs

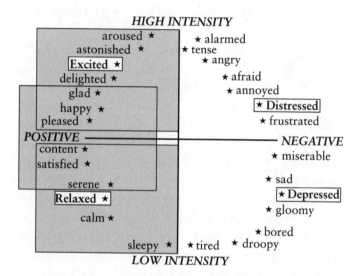

Source: Russell, J. A. (1980). A circumplex model of affect. *Journal of Personality and Social Psychology, 39,* 1161–1178. Copyright © 1980 by the American Psychological Association. Adapted with permission.

neutral or positive events. Especially disconcerting for sport participants, negative events encourage more *paralysis by analysis* than do positive events. In other words, when feeling negative about a situation or event, we tend to analyze it to death. We want to figure out why it's occurring and how to fix it. This saps energy and redirects attention away from the task at hand into other things. This can pose serious problems for golfers.

Some elaboration and examples may help under-line this important point. In 1932, Walter Cannon described these effects of negative events as the "fight-or-flight reaction." Cannon proposed that when an organism perceives a threat, the body rapidly mobilizes its resources to handle it. After all, as hunters and gatherers, our ancestors were exposed to dangerous situations on a regular basis. This is why our nervous and endocrine systems have the ability to secrete biochemicals called *catecholamines* rapidly into the bloodstream to increase heart rate, blood pressure, blood sugar levels, and breathing rate. These biological reactions put the organism into a state of readiness to attack the threat or to run away from it. These same biological reactions occur even when people are exposed to opinions that disagree with their own. Positive events do not impose such immediate threats. Therefore, our biological systems do not immediately prepare us to handle good feelings.

Negative events also narrow the range of attention and greatly increase thinking about such events. We have a more elaborate terminology for describing negative aspects of our lives than positive ones. We also spend a great deal of energy trying to solve problems and change negative states into more positive states.

Another mechanism by which negative moods create problems for golfers concerns effects on tentativeness and anxiety. Negative moods increase perceptions of dangers of all kinds, not merely those that gave rise to the negative mood in the first place. Consider the effects of a negative mood stemming from a poor shot. If that negative mood becomes powerful, it will stay with you. As you go to hit the recovery shot, you may exaggerate the risks around you and have greater difficulty committing to that recovery shot. How can you commit 100 percent if your negative mood creates this darkened cloud that prevents you from believing in yourself? Poor commitment also creates tentativeness in the swing, making it more mechanical and less smooth and automatic. Golfers clearly need methods that help them stay positive and thereby stay capable of playing the game with confidence.

Techniques to Maintain Positivity

Several ideas and techniques can help you stay in your ZOF. These techniques combat the inherent negativity of golf. You will find that using them can help you school your temper, bringing you closer to the cheerful state that Whigham implored us to strive toward in golf and "in all relations of life." They will also help you shoot lower numbers.

You can trace your emotional state on the golf course to how you felt when you woke up or perhaps to feelings on the day or week before you started playing. Some observers would argue you could trace your feelings back to your early childhood. To stay more practical, this section focuses on techniques you can use as you are playing a round of golf. Certainly this does not negate the arguments on preparation in Chapter Two. If you give yourself enough time to prepare before a round of golf, you set the stage for maintaining control of your emotional states. Yet no matter how well you prepare in advance, you can still use some methods during the game to combat the natural negativity that comes from playing golf with less than perfect skills.

The *React* Rule

Do you currently set any goals for your own verbal reactions (and even internal reactions to yourself) as you play? We've met very few golfers who could identify such a rule. Nonetheless, adopting the following rule as a standard for your own emotional reactions can, just by itself, significantly improve your positivity on the golf course:

Keep all comments about yourself positive. This includes comments about your golf skills and about your character and intelligence. It's OK to make an occasional negative covert (internal) remark, but replace it quickly with a positive remark. Keep negative remarks as few and far between as possible—and keep them to yourself.

This is a difficult rule to follow for most golfers. Can you think, for example, of the last time you played an entire round of golf without once uttering a negative comment out loud about yourself or your skills? This includes saying things like

"What a stupid shot!"
"I just can't putt at all today."
"God, that was ugly!"
"Do you believe I hit that horrible thing?"
"Now, that was very bright!"

You may recognize these and many of their permutations and combinations. Some people think that by expressing such feelings they will somehow diffuse them. Actually, in most cases, you will magnify the negativity if you indulge in derisive expressions during sport performance. A study by sport psychologist Judy Van Raalte and her colleagues (1994) demonstrated this point by analyzing the way twenty-four competitive junior tennis players talked to themselves during important matches. These researchers found that losers of close matches used negative self-talk almost twice as frequently as winners. They also found that the players tended to use negative self-talk far more frequently than positive self-talk. For example, 88 percent of the players used negative self-talk thirteen or more times during their matches, while only 21 percent of the players used positive or instructional self-talk that often.

What if your partner or an opponent makes a negative comment about your game or your attitude? How would you react to the following?

"You are really struggling on the greens today."
"You're chipping is really off today."
"You can't seem to buy a putt today."
"I've never seen you mis-hit so many tee shots."

You could either ignore these comments or respond to them. We think it works best to respond to such comments—if only to keep them from recurring. We suggest defending your game in a simple and direct manner, for example:

"My putting is OK today. Everyone misses some of them."
"They'll start dropping for me today; you can count on it."
"I've had some challenging putts today that would give anyone a hard time."
"My swing feels pretty good. The outcomes will come around."
"Did you see the one I made on Hole X?"
"Did you see the shot I hit on Hole X? There are more where that came from."

Notice the use of positive focusing to redirect your playing partner's attention. You can also specifically point out one or two of your better shots to your playing partner or friend on subsequent holes. Another possible response is something like "I'd rather stay focused on positives or what I'm doing well." This is an even more direct statement showing your intention to stay positive no matter what.

You may find it quite difficult to adhere to this rule, particularly when you first try applying it. All you can do if it's a struggle is to keep trying. Also, you can keep trying to use positive focusing and other techniques to make this approach easier. Another idea along these lines is to tell a playing partner or friend or spouse you play with regularly that you're setting this rule in place before the round. That kind of public commitment tends to increase motivation to stay with this goal. It also may help align your playing partners so that they will be less likely to make negative comments to you. Remember, if you don't set a goal like the React Rule, it will be much harder to achieve your ZOF.

Adaptive Attributions

Back in 1886, Horace Hutchinson wrote:

> If you are one of the many golfers who overrate their game, and, when constantly beaten by those

they imagined to be their inferiors, are in the habit ascribing their ill-success to indisposition, the state of the atmosphere, or even to the Government's foreign policy or the spots on the sun, you really must not be surprised at finding some ill-natured persons disposed to accept the issue of a large number of matches as a terribly conclusive test of your powers, in preference to attributing the result to any agency in the field of politics or astronomy.

[Moreover], do not get into the habit of pointing out the particularly salient blade of grass which you imagined to have been the cause of your failing to hole your putt. . . . The opinion of a man who has just missed his putt, about the state of that particular putting green, is usually accepted with some reserve.

Hutchinson counseled against attributing problems in your golf game to such external forces as sunspots or errant blades of grass on a putting green. A more modern version of this opinion was expressed by the revered Austin teaching professional, Harvey Penick: "I think it is fine to get mad if you hit a poor shot or miss a putt you should have made. Getting mad shows that you have the competitive spirit. . . . In your mind call yourself every name you can think of for the poor shot that you just hit. But while you are being mad, be mad only at yourself . . . and don't be mad at luck. Stick to the one thing you can control: you."

Hutchinson's and Penick's folk wisdom argues in favor of taking full responsibility for the events that befall you on the golf course. Yet can you remember a single instance of Jack Nicklaus analyzing a round of golf in which he blamed himself for missing a putt or shot? Nicklaus usually attributes mis-hits to such things as spike marks or gusts of wind or some other external factor. How many times have you seen Steve Ballesteros and even Tiger Woods look indignantly to the throngs surrounding them for someone who moved or clicked a photo—as an explanation for their mis-hit shots? Can such external distractions really account for all of their mis-hits?

Some people argue that no-fault golf is a cop-out. Others believe that such attributions are adaptive and very helpful. Science favors the no-fault approach. This approach to attributing causes of problems to external factors leads to a less depressed and more optimistic approach to the game.

Let's take a step back at this point and consider more carefully the definition of attributions. Then we will revisit the Nicklaus no-fault-style attributions and compare them to the alternatives.

Attributions are beliefs about the causes of behavior. These beliefs assign responsibility for actions, events, or thoughts. Attributions vary along three dimensions:

Internal ——————— External
Stable ——————— Unstable
Global ——————— Specific

Internal attributions ascribe causes of events to oneself. This follows Penick's advice precisely: "I just missed a four-foot putt. It's my fault. It's something within me, such as my skill level or my ability to handle pressure that caused the missed putt." In contrast, external attributions assign the primary cause for events to others or the environment. When looking at that missed putt, I could say that it was derailed by a spike mark or an irregularity in the putting surface. I could also blame the pressure of the situation for the missed putt. Viewing the pressure as problematic places some of the blame for the missed putt on the external world, not my own problems handling the external world.

Stable attributions are those that remain relatively constant over time. I could, for example, describe myself as a poor putter as a way of explaining why I missed that putt. Variations on that conclude: "I just don't play well in the morning." "I always have trouble in the afternoons." "I can't ever read these greens right." More unstable attributions, in contrast, imply that changes will occur over time. Examples of unstable attributions include: "I'm just having trouble putting today." "I've been feeling a lot of pressure these last couple of days."

"I can't quite get the line on these putts in the last couple of weeks."

Global attributions assign responsibility for events in very general terms. For example, what if you had practiced in the last couple of weeks and yet still didn't score better than your average on a particular day. You could decide that your game stayed the same because "life isn't fair" or "that's just the way it is." More specific attributions suggest looking for details when assigning responsibilities, for example, "One score does not determine a general trend in performance." "Perhaps my practice didn't focus enough on ways of scoring better." "Although I practiced these last two weeks, perhaps I didn't practice enough."

The most helpful attributions keep you hopeful, not depressed. Attributions that increase depression are those that are internal, global, and stable. If you believe that the problems in your golf game are caused by something that is very much a part of you (internal), that won't change over time (stable), and that is hard to pin down (global), you may not work hard to improve your game. Examples of these internal, stable, and global attributions include: "I just don't have what it takes to play this game." "I can't focus well enough to play golf effectively." "I can't master this game because I started playing it when I was too old."

Attributions that are external, unstable, and specific promote hope, for example: "These greens are tough (external, specific) to read today (unstable)." "Anyone would have to practice putting (external) more than I have lately (unstable) to score better than I did today (specific)."

Searching for external, unstable, and specific causes promotes a problem-solving attitude. You want to avoid attributing difficulties on the golf course to some fundamental aspect of your character or abilities. Instead, find ways of identifying specific problems in your game that you believe can change if you practice effectively enough or get the right kind of help to make that change. External, unstable, and specific attributions argue that change is possible. Internal, stable, and global attributions suggest that change is impossible. We think that using external, unstable, and specific attributions actually takes more responsibility for the quality of your golf game than blaming yourself per se for your problems in golf.

The 4-F Technique

Lisa was playing a pretty good round on her home course. She was in her usual Sunday foursome. She got to the reasonably easy par 5 fifteenth hole. She realized that she had no chance of getting to the green in two, so she wisely opted for a 5-wood off the tee. She hit a good shot. The ball went about 180 yards. It was in the light rough on the right side of the fairway—no major problem and in pretty good shape. She elected to hit another 5-wood second shot to leave herself about 120 yards from the middle of the green, if she hit it well. She hit her second ball pretty much like the first. Once again, she found herself in the light rough—this time on the left side, nothing major in her way. She had an open shot of about 125 yards to an accessible pin placement on the right side of the green.

As she strolled up toward her ball, she was feeling good about the situation. She noticed two of her playing partners were in pretty good shape, but the third (Sue) was struggling mightily. "Fortunately, Sue's not on my team!" Lisa thought. As Lisa was approaching her ball, she began studying the lie and deciding what kind of shot to hit into this green. She decided on a 9-iron. She went through her usual preshot routine. She was feeling confident and was looking forward to a good chance at par. Everything felt good about the swing except when the club hit only the top half of the ball, skulling it short and way left of the green. "I can't believe I topped that shot," she muttered angrily. Now what?

Lisa faced a choice almost every golfer confronts during almost every round of golf. She could give herself a good chance for a scrambling par by knocking the next shot onto the green in good shape. Or she could turn one problem into another problem. What would you do?

The 4-F Technique (Kirschenbaum, 1997) could help Lisa increase her chances of following a problem with a success. The 4 F's are:

Fudge!
Fix
Forget
Focus

The first F—Fudge!—encourages Lisa to express herself, briefly and preferably silently, if she feels that strongly about the shot. You may recall that the React rule encourages golfers to avoid such negative reactions, if possible. Sometimes these reactions are unavoidable. Even if Lisa can't keep herself from having some reaction to this problem, she can at least minimize the damages by using the 4-F Technique. She can just allow the reaction to occur without feeling guilty about it. But she needs to make it brief. Tantrums, club throwing, extended cursing, and whining exaggerate the problem—and would keep her emotions too negative. Such outbursts also distract and annoy playing partners.

After Lisa lamented her "worm burner," it was time to move on. She expressed herself briefly so now she could proceed to the second F, Fix. Fix encourages you to take a practice swing from the place where the problematic shot occurred. Try to make some change in your approach to that shot and then actually swing to show yourself that you can fix it. Lisa did this; she stepped away and thought about what she usually did when she topped the ball. "I tend to make only a partial turn, I don't complete my turn when I top the ball."

Then she made a practice swing in which she completed her turn. "That felt more like it," she said to herself with a smile.

After convincing herself that she could fix the problem, Lisa quickly moved the third F, *F*orget. Lisa reminded herself that "no one plays golf perfectly." "Everyone tops a shot now and then." "I could use more practice out of the rough so I don't alter my approach in the rough the next time around." A relevant golf saying we encourage players to remember is "Savor the ones you like; replace the ones you don't."

After replacing her problematic shot, Lisa proceeded to the final F, *F*ocus. During Focus, you attempt to direct your attention to the next shot in a positive and optimistic manner. You try to stay with your usual preshot routine and go through those motions with a sense of confidence and eagerness. Lisa started on this before she even reached her ball. She saw the ball lying in medium rough behind a bunker. She thought to herself, "This is an interesting shot." She realized that she had practiced this type of flop wedge in recent weeks and really liked the shot. She got herself to look forward to trying it out in this situation, remembering her success. As she approached the ball, she preceded to identify a specific target, use imagery, and then go through her usual preshot routine.

You can see how the 4-F Technique integrates other aspects of *R*eact. It systematically helps downplay problematic shots. It gives you something to do other than stew about some of the challenges in golf. It encourages you to take a practice swing to bring some closure on the problematic shot. If you just mis-hit one, the best way to convince yourself that it won't happen again is to take a practice swing in a similar situation and use imagery and other techniques to see the outcome much improved. You can certainly use adaptive attributions and other positive ways of talking to yourself in the Forget phase of this approach. You can also use the Focus element to bring yourself back into focusing on a specific target and on the use of your full preshot routine.

Real-Life Focus

Bobby Jones didn't have the advantage of the research behind the principles described in this chapter. He never heard of Zones of Optimal Functioning or the 4-F Technique. Yet he discovered on his own that perfection in golf was unattainable, even for him. He had to develop methods of coping with problematic shots so that he could focus and stay optimistic.

Bobby Jones described the coping self-talk he used extremely well three years before accomplishing what *Golf World* recently identified as the most remarkable accomplishment in the last fifty years in golf, his 1930 Grand Slam:

In the seven years between 1916 and 1922, inclusive, I played in eleven national championships and did not win one. In the four years including 1923 and 1926, I played in ten national championships, winning five and finishing second three times. . . .

There has been a change in my tournament attitude; of that I am sure. It was not an improvement in shot-making. Leaving off the minor refinements, I had as good an assortment shots in the seven lean years as I have today. I think I never played particularly badly in any of those tournaments, before I broke through to win. . . .

I began to understand that the other fellows had their troubles, too; that I didn't have to go out and shoot four perfect rounds to win a major open championship, or even one perfect round, if I could just keep four decent rounds sticking together. I suppose I began instinctively to understand that one lost stroke did not necessarily have to be redeemed at once; perhaps it was not ruinous; perhaps the other fellows were losing a stroke, too. . . .

So maybe that is the answer—the stolid and negative and altogether unromantic attribute of patience. It is nothing new or original to say that golf is played one stroke at a time. But it took me many years to realize it. And it's easy to forget, now [Jones and Keeler, 1927].

A more modern example is the reaction of a teaching professional who learned how to use Smart Golf.

She had played very little in the year or so prior to taking the seminar, because golf had become increasingly frustrating to her. The seminar turned things around:

> Smart Golf put the fun back into golf. My swing was inefficient. My feel—I had none. Still I was able to have a good attitude because I was realistic using Smart Golf. I made, what I consider, only two good shots in 36 holes. Yet, my reactions remained good. Because of the way I played, I could have been miserable. *But,* I was not! I took each shot as it came. I kept my *P*lan, *A*pply, and *R*eact monitoring focused for the most part. I lost my temper only twice. This is not bad. I really had fun playing golf again.

The *R*eact rule, adaptive attributions, and the 4-F Technique all make it easier for mere mortals to achieve what Bobby Jones described as "the stolid and altogether unromantic attribute of patience."

Ever since golf began—Scottish stories have settled on the year 1100 as a reasonable date of birth—the game has been an enigma. For those who have steered clear of its clutches, the devotion it demands from its followers looms as one of the great absurdities of the human race's supposed progress. There are moments when all golfers agree with this verdict [Wind, 1954, p. xv].

The main point of Smart Golf is to help you become a better golfer by unlocking the secrets of your mental game. This often translates into a more consistent, and consistently positive, approach to the game. The game doesn't have to produce misery and regrets. It can provide fulfillment for the devotion it demands. It is one of the few sports that keeps giving back to you in proportion to what you give to it throughout your lifetime. We hope that the ideas in this book can help you realize that remarkable potential.

References

Chapter One: A Thirty-Minute Smart Golf Primer

Kirschenbaum, D. S. (1997). *Mind matters: Seven steps to smarter sport performance.* Carmel, IN: Cooper.

Sarazen, G. (1950). It takes brains to play golf. In G. Sarazen with H. W. Wind, *Thirty years of championship golf.* Upper Saddle River, NJ: Prentice Hall.

Chapter Two: Preparation

Balfour, A. J. (1954). Some of the humors of golf. In H. W. Wind (Ed.), *The complete golfer.* New York: Simon & Schuster. (Originally published in 1890.)

Smollet, T. (1954). The links of Leith. In H. W. Wind (Ed.), *The complete golfer.* New York: Simon & Schuster. (Originally published in 1890.)

Chapter Three: Positive Focusing

Johnston-O'Connor, E. J., & Kirschenbaum, D. S. (1986). Something succeeds like success: Positive self-monitoring for unskilled golfers. *Cognitive Therapy and Research, 10,* 123–136.

Kirschenbaum, D. S., & Bale, R. M. (1980). Cognitive-behavioral skills in golf: Brain power golf. In R. M. Suinn (Ed.), *Psychology in sports: Methods and applications.* Minneapolis, MN: Burgess.

Nicklaus, J. (1974). *Golf my way.* New York: Simon & Schuster.

Chapter Four: Plan

Azar, B. (1996, Nov.). Psychologists have preliminary results on the most comprehensive research project on middle age. *American Psychological Association Monitor,* p. 26.

Demaret, J. (1954). *My partner, Ben Hogan.* New York: McGraw-Hill.

Eysenck, N. W. (1993). *Principles of cognitive psychology.* Hillsdale, NJ: Erlbaum.

Jenkins, D. (1994). *Fairways and greens: The best golf writing of Dan Jenkins.* New York: Doubleday.

Jones, R. T. (1954). Introduction. In H. W. Wind (Ed.), *The complete golfer.* New York: Simon & Schuster. (Originally published in 1890.)

Kahneman, D., Slovic, P., & Tversky, A. (1982). *Judgment under uncertainty: Heuristics and biases.* New York: Cambridge University Press.

McCord, G., & Kostis, P. (1996, Dec.). A lesson from the dark side. *Golf Digest,* p. 40.

Nisbett, R. E. (Ed.). (1993). *Rules for reasoning.* Hillsdale, NJ: Erlbaum.

Nisbett, R. E., & Ross, L. (1980). *Human inference: Strategies and shortcomings of social judgment.* Upper Saddle River, NJ: Prentice Hall.

Taylor, S. E., & Brown, J. D. (1988). Illusion and well-being: A social-psychological perspective on mental health. *Psychological Bulletin, 103,* 193–210.

Weist, N. D., Finney, J. W., & Ollendick, T. H. (1992, November). Cognitive biases in child behavior therapy. *The Behavior Therapist,* pp. 249–252.

Chapter Five: Apply

Boutcher, S. H., & Zinsser, N. W. (1990). Cardiac deceleration of the elite and beginning golfers during putting. *Journal of Sport and Exercise Psychology, 12,* 37–47.

Crews, D. J., & Boutcher, S. H. (1986). An exploratory, observational behavior analysis of professional golfers during competition. *Journal of Sport Behavior, 9,* 51–58.

Hanley, R. (1994, June 12). Paying the price for fame. *Chicago Tribune.*

Kluger, A. N., & De Nise, A. (1996). The effects of feedback interventions on performance: A historical review, a meta-analysis, and a preliminary feedback intervention theory. *Psychological Bulletin, 119,* 254–284.

Nelson, L. R., & Furst, M. L. (1972). An objective study of the effects of expectation on competitive performance. *Journal of Psychology, 81,* 69–72.

Sarazen, G. (1950). It takes brains to play golf. In G. Sarazen with H. W. Wind, *Thirty years of championship golf.* Upper Saddle River, NJ: Prentice Hall.

Singer, R. N., Lidor, R., & Cauraugh, J. H. (1993). To be aware or not aware? What to think about while learning and performing a motor skill. *The Sport Psychologist, 7,* 19–30.

Swing keys of the 1996 major champions. (1997, January). *Golf Digest,* pp. 71–81.

Travis, W. J. (1910, March). How I won the British Amateur Championship. *American Golfer.*

Zimmerman, B. (in press). Self-regulation of motoric learning: A strategic cycle view. *Journal of Applied Sport Psychology.*

Chapter Six: React and the 4-F Technique

Cannon, W. (1932). *The wisdom of the body.* New York: Norton.

Hanin, Y. L. (1980). The study of anxiety in sports. In W. F. Straub (Ed.), *Sport psychology: An analysis of athlete behavior.* Ithaca, NY: Mouvement.

Hutchinson, H. G. (1954). Hints to golfers of riper years. In H. W. Wind (Ed.), *The complete golfer.* New York: Simon & Schuster. (Originally published in 1890.)

Jones, R. T, Jr., & Keeler, O. B. (1927). *Down the fairway.* New York: Minton Balch.

Kirschenbaum, D. S. (1997). *Mind matters: Seven steps to smarter sport performance.* Carmel, IN: Cooper.

Penick, H., with Shrake, B. (1992). *Harvey Penick's little red book: Lessons and teachings from a lifetime in golf.* New York: Simon & Schuster.

Russell, J. A. (1980). A circumplex model of affect. *Journal of Personality and Social Psychology, 39,* 1161–1178.

Van Raalte, J. L., Brewer, B. W., Rivera, P. M., & Petipas, A. J. (1994). The relationship between observable self-talk and competitive junior tennis players' match performances. *Journal of Sport and Exercise Psychology, 16,* 400–415.

Whigham, H. J. (1986). The common sense of golf. In M. Shapiro, W. Dohn, & L. Berger (Eds.). *Golf: A turn-of-the-century treasury.* Secaucus, NJ: Castle. (Original work published 1910)

Wind, H. W. (1954). *The story of American golf: Its champions and its championships.* New York: Simon & Schuster.

Recommended Reading

Cochran, A. J., & Farrally, M. R. (Eds.). (1994). *Science and golf II: Proceedings of the World Scientific Congress of Golf.* London: Spon.

Kirschenbaum, D. S. (1997). *Mind matters: Seven steps to smarter sport performance.* Carmel, IN: Cooper.

Murphy, S. (1996). *The achievement zone: An eight-step guide to peak performance in all arenas of life.* New York: Berkeley Books.

Owens, D., & Bunker, L. K. (1992). *Advanced golf: Steps to success.* Champaign, IL: Human Kinetics.

Owens, D., & Bunker, L. K. (1995). *Golf: Steps to success* (2nd ed.). Champaign, IL: Human Kinetics.

Snead, S., & Tarde, J. (1986). *Pigeon marks, hustlers and other golf bettors you can beat.* Trumbull, CT: Golf Digest.

Williams, J. M. (Ed.). (1993). *Applied sport psychology: Personal growth to peak performance* (2nd ed.). Mountain View, CA: Mayfield.

Van Raalte, J. L., & Brewer, B. W. (Eds.). (1996). *Exploring sport and exercise psychology.* Washington, DC: American Psychological Association.

About the Authors

DEDE OWENS is a teaching professional at Cog Hill Golf Club in Lemont, Illinois, and a member of Callaway Golf Company's Instructional Advisory Staff and the *Golf Digest* Professional Advisory Staff. A former professional on the Ladies Professional Golf Association (LPGA) Tour, she holds the LPGA's Master Teaching ranking. She was selected as the Midwest Teacher of the Year five times (1989–1993) and the National LPGA Teacher of the Year twice (1978, 1993). She is the national president of the LPGA Teaching Division (1994 to present).

In 1985, Dr. Owens received the Joe Graffis Award from the National Golf Foundation for her "outstanding contribution to golf education." This contribution has been made not only through her work as a teaching professional but also through her teaching at the University of North Carolina, Delta State University, Illinois State University, and the University of Virginia. She is also a coauthor of five other books on golf, including the best-selling book in colleges, *Golf: Steps to Success* (2nd ed., 1995), and is a coauthor of eight research studies on golf. She was recently included in the *Golf Magazine* listing of the top one hundred teaching professionals in golf.

DAN KIRSCHENBAUM is director of the Center for Behavioral Medicine in Chicago, Illinois, and professor of psychiatry and behavioral sciences at Northwestern University. He has provided keynote addresses at all three of North America's professional societies for sport psychologists. He has written seven books and a hundred articles for scientific journals and books. Dr. Kirschenbaum is a fellow and former president of the largest organization of sport psychologists in the world, the American Psychological Association's Division of Exercise and Sport Psychology. He is also a fellow and one of the founders of the second-largest organization for sport psychologists, the Association for the Advancement of Applied Sport Psychology (AAASP). Dr. Kirschenbaum was also appointed by the U.S. Olympic Committee to direct the Sport Psychology Team at the 1991 U.S. Olympic Festival and to serve as one of five members of the committee's Sport Psychology Advisory Group (1994 to present).

Although he has consulted with athletes from many different sports, he is best known for his research with golfers. He provided invited addresses about golf at the First International Symposium on Sport Psychology (Monterrey, Mexico—1978) and at the Second World

Scientific Congress on Golf (St. Andrews, Scotland—1994). Dr. Kirschenbaum practices what he has studied (although not very much during Chicago's long winters)—he was the number two "man" on his high school golf team, is a three-time winner or winning team member of the AAASP annual golf tournament, and maintains a single-digit handicap.

Index